The Dallas Morning News

HOW 'BOUT THEM COWBOYS!

THE RETURN OF AMERICA'S TEAM

ANDREWS AND McMEEL

A Universal Press Syndicate Company

KANSAS CITY

The Dallas Morning News

PUBLISHER AND EDITOR
Burl Osborne

SENIOR VICE PRESIDENT AND EXECUTIVE EDITOR
Ralph Langer

DEPUTY MANAGING EDITOR/ EXECUTIVE SPORTS EDITOR
Dave Smith

ASSISTANT MANAGING EDITOR/VISUALS
John Davidson

NEWS ART DIRECTOR
Ed Kohorst

BOOK DESIGN
Edna Jamandre

COPY CHIEF
Mike Hashimoto

PHOTO EDITORS
Catharine Krueger
John F. Rhodes

TEXT
Frank Luksa

PHOTOGRAPHERS
Donna Bagby
Louis DeLuca
Tom Fox
Juan Garcia
Ken Geiger
Randy Eli Grothe
Steve Hamm
Carolyn Herter
Milton Hinnant
Paula Nelson
David Pellerin
Richard Michael Pruitt
John F. Rhodes
Erich Schlegel
William Snyder
Irwin Thompson
David Woo
Cindy Yamanaka

COPY EDITING
Terry Bigham
Mike Hamilton
Joe Jansen
Mark Johnson
Rob Stroope

PHOTO PRODUCTION
Patricia Chase
Margaret Eastman
Gladys Golden
Leila Hill

There is a saying that what goes around comes around. The Dallas Cowboys grabbed football's brass ring in the 1970s and lost it completely in the 1980s. Now, they are back. This book by *The Dallas Morning News* staff is an exciting chronicle, in words and pictures, of the return to prominence of the most popular football team in America.

Burl Osborne
Publisher and editor
The Dallas Morning News

ISBN: 0-8362-8062-1

Library of Congress Catalog Card Number: 93-70466

CONTENTS

TRANSITION TEAM H.R. "Bum" Bright (above) announces the transfer of ownership in the Cowboys to Arkansas business-man Jerry Jones (seated). In the background is Tex Schramm, the team's president and general manager for its first 29 years. That Feb. 25, 1989, news conference was one day after Jones and Jimmy Johnson were spotted in Dallas eating at Mia's (right), coincidentally Tom Landry's favorite Tex-Mex restaurant. The irony of that photograph, splashed across the front page of *The Dallas Morning News,* did not ease the transition for the new owner and coach.

REVIVAL OF THE DALLAS COWBOYS began with relapse. Things got worse before better, then got better than anyone could have imagined.

The Cowboys' pendulum forever swings. It just never stops on center.

This franchise is a collection of extreme personalities, extravagant defeats and victories, in style and substance apart from all others. It is its birthright to be different, its fate to be unique and its tradition to operate with flair.

Nothing in sports succeeds like excess, and the Cowboys have been excessively dramatic since joining the NFL as expansion members in 1960. Few moments in their history were more dramatic than Feb. 25, 1989.

Revival began with the last rites for the only head coach the franchise had known. Tom Landry was fired. President and general manager Tex Schramm's forced exit followed. Scouting director Gil Brandt, the final member of a troika intact for 29 years, also was swept aside.

These men of the Old Era had lifted the Cowboys from a maiden 0-11-1 poorhouse to the NFL pinnacle: 20 consecutive winning seasons, two Super Bowl titles in a then-record five appearances and mystique spawning the envied compliment of "America's Team."

On that Feb. 25, the Cowboys became the possession of an oilman stranger from Arkansas. They were Jerry Jones' team now, transferred for $140 million from an 11-man limited partnership headed by Dallas businessman H.R. "Bum" Bright.

Revival had begun. It led onward and upward toward a peak once believed impossible to scale. The 1992 Cowboys would win more games (16) than the 1989 Cowboys lost (15).

The '92 campaign unfolded as if a magic carpet ride. First came a 13-3 regular season void of major crisis in terms of injury or must-win game. Then three playoff contests the Cowboys won by 24, 10 and 35 points.

They went over the top in the last one, Super Bowl XXVII against Buffalo at the Rose Bowl in Pasadena, Calif. The score was 52-17 and not that close.

But relapse preceded revival, and distant replay is required to remind of the depths from which a world champion evolved.

★

The first team of the New Era regressed to a 1-15 record from the 3-13 plight it inherited. Yet Jones had made a choice that would transport him from a local figure of folly to a ticker-tape parade down Commerce Street as the owner of pro football's world champion.

The most important decision of his tenure? "It's pretty easy," he said. "The first one, when I hired Jimmy Johnson to be the coach."

Jones' former teammate and road roommate on the University of Arkansas' 1964 national champion, Johnson had coached the University of Miami to a 52-9 record, including a 1987 national championship. He made a shocking discovery upon arriving in the NFL. He had left more skill behind.

"I was disappointed," he said. "I'd always held the Cowboys in such high regard, almost on a pedestal. I was a little dismayed at what I saw on the field. I'd just come from a (college) team that had more talent."

Was it *that* bad?

"The talent level was not only marginal," he said, "it was below what the rest of the league was playing with."

Jones, meanwhile, got off on the wrong foot in Dallas. He kept putting it in his mouth, managing to offend just about everyone with his case of trap tongue.

Feminists howled when he spoke of the Dallas Cowboys Cheerleaders as being "the pick of the litter." Eyebrows arched when he said quarterback Troy Aikman "looked good in the shower." Grammar students swooned when Jones made use of a new word, "uncomfortableness."

This was the moment of total relapse. A 1-15 team. A college coach who looked over his

ALL-TIME RECORDS

Year	W	L	T	Playoff finish*
1960	0	11	1	None
1961	4	9	1	None
1962	5	8	1	None
1963	4	10	0	None
1964	5	8	1	None
1965	7	7	0	None
1966	10	3	1	Lost NFL title game
1967	9	5	0	Lost NFL title game
1968	12	2	0	Lost Eastern title game
1969	11	2	1	Lost Eastern title game
1970	10	4	0	Lost Super Bowl V
1971	11	3	0	Won Super Bowl VI
1972	10	4	0	Lost NFC title game
1973	10	4	0	Lost NFC title game
1974	8	6	0	None
1975	10	4	0	Lost Super Bowl X
1976	11	3	0	Lost divisional playoff
1977	12	2	0	Won Super Bowl XII
1978	12	4	0	Lost Super Bowl XIII
1979	11	5	0	Lost divisional playoff
1980	12	4	0	Lost NFC title game
1981	12	4	0	Lost NFC title game
1982	6	3	0	Lost NFC title game
1983	12	4	0	Lost wild-card game
1984	9	7	0	None
1985	10	6	0	Lost divisional playoff
1986	7	9	0	None
1987	7	8	0	None
1988	3	13	0	None
1989	1	15	0	None
1990	7	9	0	None
1991	11	5	0	Lost divisional playoff
1992	13	3	0	Won Super Bowl XXVII

W-L-T for regular season only.
* Does not include Playoff Bowl games after the 1968 and '69 seasons.

JERRY JONES

On the most important decision of his tenure:

"It's pretty easy. The first one, when I hired Jimmy Johnson to be the coach."

JIMMY JOHNSON

On the team he inherited in 1989:

"I'd always held the Cowboys in such high regard, almost on a pedestal. I was a little dismayed at what I saw on the field. I'd just come from a (college) team that had more talent ... The talent level was not only marginal, it was below what the rest of the league was playing with."

BUDDY RYAN

Needling Jimmy Johnson about his college background:

"Tell him that there won't be any East Carolinas on his schedule."

head in the NFL. An owner who made dopey statements, including a brag that Johnson was worth five No. 1 draft choices and five Heisman Trophy winners. A critic quickly recommended Jones trade Johnson for his alleged worth before sundown.

Buddy Ryan, then coaching the Philadelphia Eagles, tossed a barb at Johnson's college background. "Tell him," Ryan needled, "that there won't be any East Carolinas on his schedule."

Yet unknown except to those involved, Johnson twice had been sounded out about coaching the Cowboys. Brandt made contact in 1987 to gauge his mood in becoming an aide to Landry with the implication that he would be in place as the heir apparent. Johnson declined.

The next year, Schramm called Johnson upon hearing rumors that Philadelphia was close to dumping Ryan and had cast an Eagle eye on the Miami coach. Schramm wished to learn of Johnson's interest in that job and, with Landry's career winding down, explore the options for his possible successor.

No offer or promise was made, but Schramm remembers Johnson's reaction to the prospect of one day coaching the Cowboys. "He said it was his life's ambition," Schramm said.

Football is the business and pleasure of Johnson's life to the exclusion of all else. He is laser-intent, tunnel-vision fixed on the game to the point of needing or wanting few close personal relationships.

A smattering of observers have scolded him for being overly consumed with football. To which Johnson replies: "What's wrong with wanting to be not only good, but the best, and willing to work to get there?"

Johnson turned the Cowboys in that direction with the monster 1989 trade of Herschel Walker to Minnesota. The Cowboys received enough conditional draft choices to refloat the Spanish Armada, as the Vikings handed over three No. 1s, three No. 2s and a No. 3, not to mention five veteran players.

"With that many draft choices, you can't lose," said Brandt, the former draftmaster.

"Lots of people said that," Johnson rebutted, "but it's not that simple. Sure, it gave us a wonderful opportunity to get extra picks. But the Rams had the (Eric) Dickerson deal and

JOHN F. RHODES

CRACK BACK The early years of the Cowboys' New Era are not kind to quarterback Troy Aikman, who wonders at times how long he can stand the physical punishment.

got extra picks. What you do with those picks is pretty important."

Johnson did all right. Spinoff dividends from the Walker trade dotted his Super Bowl roster: Two-time NFL rushing champ Emmitt Smith; Outland Trophy winner Russell Maryland; rookie Kevin Smith, starting at left corner in place of Issiac Holt, one of the five former Vikings veterans; Darren Woodson and Clayton Holmes, waiting in the secondary wings and playing key roles on the nickel pass defense and special teams.

Johnson thereafter made 40-odd more trades, shopped the Plan B market and drafted wisely. He displayed a talent for knowing talent. Team fortune rose in rapid increments from 1-15 to 7-9 to 11-5 and a wild-card playoff berth last season, the Cowboys' first post-season trip since 1985.

He also was lucky. Poor as his on-field inheritance may have been, he did fall into the No. 1 choice in a 1989 draft of extraordinary vintage. It produced the rarest of grapes: the Franchise Quarterback who would mature into the Most Valuable Player of Super Bowl XXVII.

Aikman was a no-brainer choice then and is now a brain-lock cinch to become the NFL's dominant quarterback, if he isn't already. No team extracted a skill of relevant magnitude since the 1983 draft brought forth John Elway and Dan Marino. Nor has a quarterback near Aikman's equal appeared since 1989.

"There's no question Troy is the finest quarterback I've ever been around, and I've been around some outstanding quarterbacks at Miami," said Johnson, in indirect comparison to Vinny Testaverde, Steve Walsh, Craig Erickson and Gino Torretta.

★

Assembling talent had been Johnson's first priority. Next came the hard part – his demanding work ethic.

"That is no reflection on the past," he said. "Everyone works hard, but, I mean, transferring it to the players… The first year or two, people were taken aback by the way we worked.

"The reason they were taken aback was reaction to what they were accustomed to, what had been. I'm a firm believer that hard work and enthusiasm pay dividends down the road."

Finally, Johnson surrounded himself with those of his kind. That is, assistant coaches who shared his commitment to the project.

"Bringing people into the organization who had football as the priority in their life, who had a sense of urgency to win," Johnson said. "Anyone in the organization. They all play a part."

Jones was foremost in that he had the wallet and the good sense to let Johnson pick it for player costs when necessary. The owner's tangle-tongue manner vanished. He soon proved a master of marketing and a tireless promoter.

Jones raised money on everything connected with the Cowboys: television and radio contracts, pre-season games, beer and wine sales inside Texas Stadium and outside beneath The Corral watering-hole tent. He even turned a profit on training camp by relocating from temperate Southern California to a blast-furnace in Austin.

It was following a practice there that Johnson glanced at the reams of sponsors' banners draped over a fence surrounding the field at St. Edward's University.

"This looks like a minor league baseball park," he said. Then, with a grin, "Jerry didn't get rich being dumb."

Jones' sheer energy, unflagging optimism, insistence on shaking every hand and revival-preacher willingness to spread the Cowboys' gospel to every suburban substation where a fan might buy a ticket eventually turned his image.

Texas Stadium began to sell out under the New Era as early as 1990. A new fan, more vocal than those since the mid-1960s, also emerged. The joint started to jump.

Jones played Johnny Appleseed by sowing a fresh growth of interest. The part of Johnny One-Note went to Johnson, who knew but a single key – and that was to win.

Owner and coach meshed nicely in their respective arenas. Jones was as consumed

JOHNSON'S RESUME

Jimmy Johnson's year-by-year record as a head coach:

OKLAHOMA STATE

Year	W	L	T	Post-season
1979	7	4	0	None
1980	4	7	0	None
1981	7	5	0	Independence Bowl (L)
1982	4	5	2	None
1983	8	4	0	Bluebonnet Bowl (W)
Totals	30	25	2	Bowl record: 1-1

UNIVERSITY OF MIAMI

Year	W	L	T	Post-season
1984	8	5	0	Fiesta Bowl (L)
1985	10	2	0	Sugar Bowl (L)
1986	11	1	0	Fiesta Bowl (L)
1987	12	0	0	Orange Bowl (W)
1988	11	1	0	Orange Bowl (W)
Totals	52	9	0	Bowl record: 2-3

DALLAS COWBOYS

Year	W	L	T	Post-season
1989	1	15	0	None
1990	7	9	0	None
1991	11	5	0	NFC wild card (1-1)
1992	13	3	0	NFC East champs (3-0)
Totals	33	33	0	Playoff record: 4-1

NO END IN SIGHT Reminders of the Cowboys' dismal 1989 season. Ernie Jones (above) beats Everson Walls and Vince Albritton (36) to haul in a 72-yard touchdown pass with 58 seconds to play in Phoenix's 24-20 victory at Tempe, Ariz. The Cowboys' record falls to 1-14 in December, with a 15-0 loss to the New York Giants in East Rutherford, N.J. Steve Folsom (85), trying to push the ball over the goal line, comes closest to scoring, but the replay official overrules the apparent touchdown.

with producing a championship budget as Johnson a world-class team. Neither abused the other's turf.

Johnson reckoned with the bottom line as much as the goal line when he made trades. Jones bowed to Johnson's expertise on personnel. They have known private wrangles, as strong-willed men always do, but they have been smart enough to compromise without lasting rancor.

Philosophy in place, system set and 10-year contract on file, Johnson played his next favorite game, that of the mind. Johnson earned a psychology degree at Arkansas and has remained a student of the science into middle age.

He believes in the power of suggestive thought. Much of his interplay with the team is based on a theory of positive reinforcement. He expressed its essence this way:

"Treat a person the way he is, and he will remain as he is. Treat a person as what he could or should be, and he will become what he could or should be."

Johnson believes that if by some rare occurrence he cannot coach a team to victory, he will talk it into winning. He will do so by turning fiction into fact – convincing players of the fiction that they are better than actual fact.

"I wanted to establish the belief that we were going to win almost to the point of overachieving what we realistically could accomplish," he said, after the unexpected 11-5 playoff season in '91. "It's a matter of attitude and, in some ways, almost brainwashing players – telling them time after time we'd be in the playoffs until, after a time, they began to believe it."

In the same way did Johnson train his psychological guns toward the 1992 regular-season opener against the Washington Redskins. As the Cowboys dragged their increasingly weary bodies through the pre-season grind from Austin to Tokyo to Miami and back to Austin, Johnson seized subtle control of their minds. They responded by smothering the Redskins, 23-10, that first Monday night.

"Of all the games we played," he said, "I was as confident about that one as any all year. We pointed to that game since the schedule came out.

"Every time I finished talking to players, I'd leave them with the thought, 'This is getting ready for the opening game with Washington.' I planted plenty of seeds."

Johnson's early critics have been plowed under by subsequent success. Yet, like Jones, Johnson never reacted sharply in private or public when lanced. Although personally sensitive to criticism, he turned a calculated cheek.

"Love your enemies," he said, explaining the ultimate psych. "It will drive them crazy."

Another facet of the Jones-Johnson tandem bears emphasis. Both are natural risk-takers. Jones made his stack in the riskiest of ventures. A man strikes oil or gas – or whiffs his bankroll. Johnson chose to coach, an occupation familiar to the post office for change-of-address labels. A man wins in that business or keeps U-Haul busy.

As a result of achievement in their respective fields, both are confident to the extreme. Seldom having failed, neither really considers it a conceivable consequence.

Jones rushed to buy a 3-13 team no native Texan would touch. Johnson agreed to coach before he caught sight of the decaying timber within. Jones bet the receipts of a lifetime and Johnson his reputation on their combined ability to restore the Cowboys.

A gambler's mentality – he's an ace at the blackjack table, too – serves and suits Johnson. He is willing to bet big on trades and drafts, with no fear of losing. When he does lose, as with deals for Danny Stubbs, Terrence Flagler and Alonzo Highsmith, Johnson acts smart. He folds his hand quickly.

"I'm like the guy on the trapeze," he said. "He's got to fall in the net occasionally, or nobody will come out to watch him."

Eventually there came a time when everything fit. Drafts produced. Trades paid. Plan B dominoed. Coaching excelled. Youth matured. Johnson told his players how good they were, only this time he believed it himself.

The time came sooner than anyone expected. It arrived in 1992.

There are simple reasons why. An absence of injury to star players. A team unusually focused on an objective to see how high and far it could go. A team that neither reveled in victory nor despaired in defeat. A team that grew better the longer it played. And other than

1992-93 KEY DATES

■ **April 26-27:** The Cowboys select 15 players in the NFL draft, including two first-rounders who eventually become starters, cornerback Kevin Smith and middle linebacker Robert Jones. The Cowboys agree to terms with three of their first four picks within hours of the draft.

■ **May 1:** Jerry Jones is appointed to the NFL Competition Committee by Commissioner Paul Tagliabue. Jones is the first owner to serve on the prestigious committee since the death of Cincinnati's Paul Brown.

■ **Oct. 25:** At the Los Angeles Coliseum, 91,505 fans attend the Cowboys' 28-13 victory over the Raiders. It is the largest crowd to witness a Cowboys' game.

■ **Dec. 21:** Before a national *Monday Night Football* audience, the Cowboys defeat Atlanta, 41-17, at the Georgia Dome to clinch the NFC East championship. It marks the Cowboys' first division title since 1985 and the 14th in club history.

■ **Dec. 23:** A club-record six Cowboys offensive players are selected to the Pro Bowl – quarterback Troy Aikman, wide receiver Michael Irvin, guard Nate Newton, tight end Jay Novacek, running back Emmitt Smith and center Mark Stepnoski.

■ **Dec. 27:** The Cowboys end the regular season with a 27-14 victory over the Chicago Bears at Texas Stadium. The victory is the Cowboys' 13th, setting a club record for victories in a season. Running back Emmitt Smith finishes with 1,713 rushing yards, becoming the first player to win consecutive NFL rushing titles since Eric Dickerson (1983-84).

■ **Jan. 10:** In their first home playoff game since 1983, the Cowboys beat NFC East rival Philadelphia, 34-10.

■ **Jan. 17:** The Cowboys beat San Francisco, 30-20, at Candlestick Park in the NFC Championship Game to qualify for their first Super Bowl since the 1978 season.

■ **Jan. 31:** The Cowboys use nine turnovers to rout Buffalo, 52-17, in Super Bowl XXVII at the Rose Bowl in Pasadena, Calif. The world championship is the club's first since the 1977 season.

San Francisco, NFC rivals that withered.

The regular season proved a relative walk in various NFL parks. From mid-season to the finish line – following a 20-10 victory over the Eagles in their eighth game – the Cowboys' division lead never shrank below two games.

"There was only one game in my mind that was crucial … the Philadelphia win during regular season," Johnson said. "I felt Philadelphia was putting it together. I knew they could make a run. And they'd beaten us once (31-7 in the teams' first meeting).

"That was a big win. From there on, it was a matter of jockeying to get the team mentally ready for the playoffs."

One way Johnson did this was to predict. In preparing the team, he would tell players what to expect in flow and rhythm. When the game unfolded to his forecast form, Johnson reinforced a follow-the-leader effect.

For instance, against the Los Angeles Raiders, Johnson warned his players that the Raiders would come out strong for the first half. Blunt their best shot early, he said, and they will wilt late. That is when the Cowboys would win the game.

So it happened. The Cowboys led by a point at halftime, fell behind by six early in the third quarter and scored the final 21 points to win, 28-13.

Another instance occurred before the NFC divisional playoff against Philadelphia. By now, Johnson was convinced the Cowboys were superior and could lose only if their pre-game concentration wandered.

He convinced players with this message early in the week: "I told the team to take care of business (practice) on Wednesday, Thursday and Friday, and the deal's done. They were prepared in all phases."

Someone asked about a turning point after the 34-10 victory. Johnson saw none.

"I felt like we'd win the game before it started," he said. "I felt we had the best team."

Super Bowl XXVII also played out as foretold. Johnson emphasized two factors on the eve of the kickoff. The Cowboys would wear down Buffalo with their depth, as they had the Raiders. And the Bills would lose on turnovers.

"I felt with as aggressive a defense as we have – we have outstanding quickness – we'd be able to come away with some takeaways," he said. "We've been very patient offensively and been able to protect the football.

"I thought that would be a big key in the game. In fact, that's what I told our players."

★

Johnson may own advanced powers of persuasion, but not even he can talk a goat into winning the Kentucky Derby. The Cowboys didn't win the Super Bowl just by hearing their coach flap his jaw. The obvious difference lay with a listening audience composed of athletic thoroughbreds.

Most were winners in college. Aikman and Ken Norton (UCLA), Smith (Florida), Irvin and Maryland (Miami), Tony Casillas (Oklahoma), Alvin Harper (Tennessee) and even tiny Central State of Ohio product Erik Williams hailed from championship teams.

Those and others brought with them the exacting mentality of a winner. Winners can't abide losing.

"There's been a feeling around here the last two years of being hungry for more, of not being satisfied with our accomplishments," Johnson said.

He aimed a mental arrow at this inner strength. He kept predicting more and better for the Cowboys. He raised expectations higher and faster than anyone.

In '91, the announced goal was a playoff berth for a team coming off a 7-9 season. And in Johnson's words, to know "success in the playoffs," meaning the Cowboys would win at least one post-season game. Sure enough, the wild-card Cowboys went 11-5 and beat Chicago in the first round.

In '92, the goal became to win the NFC East and advance to the NFC Championship Game. Once there, anything is possible, and some things are probable, such as winning Super Bowl XXVII.

"That's what I said when the season started," Johnson said, with more than a hint of a smile. "I don't mean to say I told you so, but it's pretty close."

The Cowboys for the second time in their history had been built from mud-hut squalor to penthouse quality. The Old Era did it first, requiring 12 years to transform a bare-bones expansion roster into a Super Bowl winner.

When the Cowboys finally did win their first Super Bowl over Miami, 24-3, owner Clint Murchison Jr. wryly observed: "This is the completion of our 12-year plan."

The New Era did it in four years, albeit with more of a jump-start. Aikman, Irvin, Norton, Newton, Mark Tuinei, Jim Jeffcoat, Daryl Johnston, Mark Stepnoski and Tony Tolbert were either on hand or en route through the draft.

The New Era actually went from bottom to top in three years. The '89 season became a 1-15 forfeit to make the Walker trade. Even at that, Johnson felt the job took too long.

"There was never any doubt we would get to this point," he said, "but the concern was how long it was going to take. As I've said many times, no matter how long it was going to take, it wasn't fast enough for me."

Nevertheless, the original construction foreman rose to offer a standing ovation.

"I think it's a great job," said Schramm, now retired to his boat in Key West, Fla. "It's amazing, I would have to say."

How did the New Era do it? Schramm detailed three elements that he deemed most important:

"One, they had a quarterback to start with in Aikman.

"Second, Johnson and his staff were great evaluators of personnel. They ran a lot of people through and knew what type player they wanted and the player who fit that mold.

"The other is the great trade they made with Minnesota for Walker. That's one of the all-time great trades."

Speed was a constant element in Johnson's search. Speed makes plays and can offset errors. Defensive speed gets a player to the ball. Offensive speed keeps the ball away from others.

Hence, the Cowboys' roster filled with those who fit Johnson's ultimate requirement: playmakers. He harped on that theme almost from the day Jones hired him and repeated it so often that it became part of Cowboy-speak.

"We have a lot of playmakers," he said. "Guys that don't touch the ball can be playmakers. They can be a Maryland, Charles Haley, Thomas Everett or Newton. It can be a Casillas, who got three sacks against San Francisco.

"Much as some want to point to individuals, it's hard to single out those and say they carried us to the Super Bowl. A lot of guys did it."

So the deal was done. The magic carpet ride ascended to the top. Johnson fulfilled his stated mission: "I came here to win championships."

★

Only a peripheral issue relating to Johnson remained. His durability is a subject of railbird debate. Some wonder how long he can maintain a marathon pace.

He is 49, a coach at some level since 1965 who pushes himself hard year-round. The grind of self-inflicted pressure is constant. He can endure only a few post-season days on the beach before returning to the football harness.

Will there come a time when he doesn't return?

"Oh, there'll come a day on the beach when I'm drinking a cold beer and relaxing," he said. "I don't perceive myself coaching forever. How much longer, I don't know."

He made an oblique admission of feeling slight burnout pangs. They are infrequent and of limited duration, the accumulation of season-long stress. And shortly done away with annually.

"I don't know about burnout," he said. "I have had the same thoughts in my mind every year for the past 15 years. But four or five days in the Bahamas, and I'm cranked up and ready to go again."

Therein lies the goal for 1993. All that is left for Johnson and the Cowboys is to do it again.

TEX SCHRAMM

On the Cowboys' latest Super Bowl triumph and the factors that led to it:

"I think it's a great job. It's amazing, I would have to say. A tremendous accomplishment. ... One, they had a quarterback to start with in Aikman. Second, Johnson and his staff were great evaluators of personnel. They ran a lot of people through and knew what type player they wanted and the player who fit that mold. The other is the great trade they made with Minnesota for Walker. That's one of the all-time great trades."

MILTON HINNANT

ALREADY IN DEMAND Long before he becomes a Super Bowl MVP, Troy Aikman is a popular target at training camp in Austin for mini-cams and autograph hounds. At far right, Michael Irvin and Emmitt Smith (22) develop into close friends as Cowboys, after playing for rival colleges in Florida.

MILTON HINNANT

A TIME TO SWEAT Jimmy Johnson's simple philosophy of hard work piled on top of hard work begins to pay off. He and Troy Aikman talk strategy during one of Johnson's many "voluntary" quarterback schools (left). The off-season work turns playing for the Cowboys into a year-round stretch, as Johnson makes it clear that it's his way or go away (pages 18-19, photo by Cindy Yamanaka).

FEELING THEIR WAY Defensive assistant Bob Slowik shows Mickey Pruitt and Ken Norton the plan (above). Tommie Agee (34) carries for a short gain during the second pre-season contest against Houston. At far right, Crazy Ray uses the summer heat to work himself into mid-season form.

AUGUST 1992 The Cowboys' pre-season schedule began with *sayonara* and ended with a sigh. The best thing about everything in between?

"It's over," Coach Jimmy Johnson said.

The pre-season ran an unusually long and often rancorous course. To Johnson's immense pique, his team spent 19 hours flying to Tokyo to play the Houston Oilers in the Aug. 2 American Bowl opener. This seemed much ado for a scrimmage between teams that held training camps 75 miles apart in Central Texas.

Pre-season results found the Cowboys winners of two of five games before the Sept. 7 regular-season opener against Washington. Johnson also was left with decisions and problems requiring swift solution.

PRE-SEASON GAMES

He made a late move in that direction Aug. 27, less than a week before the final cut to 45 players. Defensive end Charles Haley came aboard via a trade with the San Francisco 49ers involving draft choices. Johnson announced Haley would start in less than two weeks against the Redskins.

"I'm like a rookie coming in here," Haley said. "I'll let the coaches set the demands on what they want me to do."

Other defensive problems would require patience. Both starting tackles, Tony Casillas (knee) and Russell Maryland (toe), would not play against the Redskins. Earlier injuries had slowed or halted progress by cornerback Kevin Smith (hamstring), a No. 1 pick, and wide receiver Jimmy Smith (broken leg), a second-rounder.

The offense was likewise unsettled by contract disputes. Tight end Jay Novacek, wide receiver Michael Irvin and center Mark Stepnoski held out of training camp in Austin. Novacek signed one day before the pre-season finale against Chicago. Irvin and Stepnoski remained without contracts until the week leading to the Washington game.

Johnson therefore played the Chicago exhibition cozy by not using defending NFL rushing champion Emmitt Smith a single down. All the better to protect his running-game meal ticket.

"I would have committed suicide if I'd put Emmitt out there and someone banged him up," Johnson said.

Elsewhere, signs were positive. Rookie Robert Jones, replacing Plan B defector Jack Del Rio at middle linebacker, looked solid enough. Johnson had put himself on a spot after letting Del Rio leave by saying the 1992 linebacking group would be "the best I've had in Dallas."

A kicking duel between another rookie, Lin Elliott of Texas Tech, and former Buffalo kickoff specialist Brad Daluiso, was not resolved until the final game. Elliott became the keeper by placing four kickoffs into the end zone and succeeding on two medium-range field goals.

Ready or not, the regular season loomed. Imperfections aside, Johnson felt the underlying strength of his roster, and he pronounced the Cowboys ready. His bull's-eye summary of things to come:

"We're a better team than a year ago."

JOHN F. RHODES

JERRY JONES

On the Cowboys' trip to Tokyo:

"One of the reasons for (NFL commissioner) Paul Tagliabue insisting we come was our popularity over here. That was not overstated. You see, the Cowboys' name speaks to the Japanese perception of America."

DAVE WANNSTEDT

On trailing Miami, 21-7, at halftime:

"We have got to mature in a hurry, and it's going to take extra practice, extra film study, whatever we can do."

JIMMY JOHNSON

After the second pre-season loss to Houston on Aug. 15:

"We're busting coverages, blowing assignments. You could put up with it a couple of weeks ago, but it's not long before we have to put things together."

RAY CHILDRESS

Houston Oilers defensive tackle, on beating the Cowboys, 17-16, at Texas Stadium without holdouts Michael Irvin, Jay Novacek and Mark Stepnoski:

"They'll need their holdouts if they want to go 11-5. If they don't (sign them), you'll be able to notice the difference in the office like tonight."

PRE-SCENES The Cowboys use the pre-season to fine tune their games. Issiac Holt blocks a punt by Denver's Daren Parker (above), a skill he would employ again during the regular season, then blitzes to sack John Elway (near right). Troy Aikman (far right, top photo) finds a passing lane against Miami, and Kenneth Gant's hard tackle separates Chicago's Mark Green from a pass.

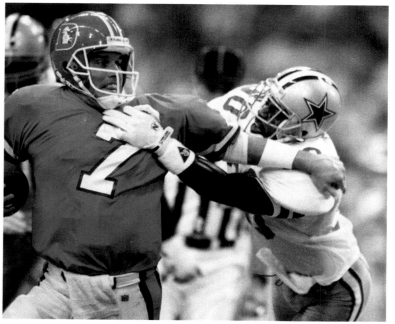

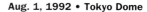

JOHN F. RHODES

Aug. 1, 1992 • Tokyo Dome

HOUSTON   34
DALLAS   23

■ Oilers' Warren Moon completes 14 of 18 passes for 134 yards and one touchdown on his two possessions.
■ Cowboys' Brad Daluiso kicks field goals of 41 and 50 yards.

Aug. 7, 1992 • Joe Robbie Stadium

DALLAS   27
MIAMI   24

■ Dan Marino completes 16 consecutive passes to give Dolphins a 21-7 halftime lead.
■ Cowboys' Alexander Wright catches two passes for 64 yards, including 51-yard touchdown.
■ Steve Beuerlein leads Cowboys' rally by completing 14 of 18 passes for 216 yards and two touchdowns.

Aug. 15, 1992 • Texas Stadium

HOUSTON   17
DALLAS   16

■ Oilers win on rookie Bucky Richardson's 22-yard touchdown pass to Wade Hopkins with 31 seconds to play.
■ Because of injuries and holdouts, Cowboys' skill-position starters are quarterback Troy Aikman, running backs Curvin Richards and Tommie Agee, wide receivers Alvin Harper and Alexander Wright and tight end Alfredo Roberts.

Aug. 22, 1992 • Texas Stadium

DALLAS   17
DENVER   3

■ Cowboys' defense records six turnovers and nine sacks.
■ Defensive end Tony Tolbert nears a three-year contract, but talks with tight end Jay Novacek break down.
■ Defensive tackles Russell Maryland (dislocated toe) and Tony Casillas (strained lower back) are injured.

Aug. 28, 1992 • Texas Stadium

CHICAGO   20
DALLAS   13

■ Defensive tackle Tony Casillas suffers sprained knee with ligament damage.
■ Charles Haley, acquired the day before from San Francisco, passes his physical but sits out the game.
■ Tight end Jay Novacek nears contract agreement, but center Mark Stepnoski rejects latest offer.

KEN GEIGER

JOHN F. RHODES

BLOCK AND ROLL Issiac Holt (above) jump-starts the Cowboys on opening night by blocking Kelly Goodburn's punt out of the end zone for a safety 3:15 into the first quarter. Ray Horton (20, right), jarring the ball loose from Redskins receiver Gary Clark, and his defensive teammates kept it going.

ERICH SCHLEGEL

SEPT. 7, 1992 • TEXAS STADIUM Storied rivalry renewed. Young challenger matured to main-event status with the Super Bowl champion. Nationally televised *Monday Night Football* stage.

Every possible element of drama meshed to lift the 1992 regular-season opener from ordinary spectacle into the realm of spectacular. No game between the Dallas Cowboys and Washington Redskins is ordinary, and this one held to historical form.

Coming on ever stronger for two seasons, the Cowboys could measure how far they had traveled. A test against the NFL's best would indicate their rate of ascent. Up, up and away they went.

Washington left Texas Stadium with its Super Bowl crown askew, with ears ringing and signals drowned by the ecstatic, sellout crowd.

DALLAS 23
WASHINGTON 10

GAME 1

The Cowboys captured a no-fluke, no-frills, 23-10 victory. The result implied the balance of power in the NFC East had shifted. Redskins coach Joe Gibbs became the first to warn that the new kid on the block appeared to have staying power.

"They are big, and they are strong, and they have good receivers," he said. "They have an excellent defense. Excellent special teams.

"I think you have to say they are a heck of a team. They really are."

Gibbs struck a prophetic chord in that the Cowboys were yet incomplete and out of sync. Michael Irvin and Jay Novacek had not shaken their holdout rust. Nor did center Mark Stepnoski sign in time to play.

Both starting defensive tackles, Russell Maryland and Tony Casillas, lay idle with injury. Those absences were early warning signs of a roster, if restored to health, that would play at an even loftier level.

The Cowboys played well enough. They scored by land, sea and air: a Troy Aikman pass, an Emmitt Smith run, a blocked punt by Ike Holt and Kelvin Martin's 79-yard punt return. A defense bearing question marks held the Redskins to a second-half field goal.

Coach Jimmy Johnson would later say he expected no less.

"Of all the games we played, I was as confident about this one as any all year," he said. "We pointed to that game as soon as the schedule came out.

"Every time I finished talking to the team, the last words they heard were something like, '...getting ready for the opening game against Washington.' I was planting those seeds early."

The first seed sprouted into a blossom. They Cowboys were on their way to smelling the flowers.

MARK RYPIEN

Redskins quarterback
"There was a lot of pressure, and the crowd noise had something to do with it."

RANDY GALLOWAY

Sept. 8 column:
Great defense in the opener leads to even greater expectations for the season.

JIMMY JOHNSON

"To beat a team like Washington you have to win all three phases."

KELVIN MARTIN

On his 79-yard punt return for a touchdown:
"I wanted to make the big play. I made some mistakes, but I tried to stay positive."

HAPPY TOGETHER
Michael Irvin (88) is the first to congratulate Alvin Harper on his 26-yard touchdown reception that gave the Cowboys a 16-7 halftime lead.

JOHN F. RHODES

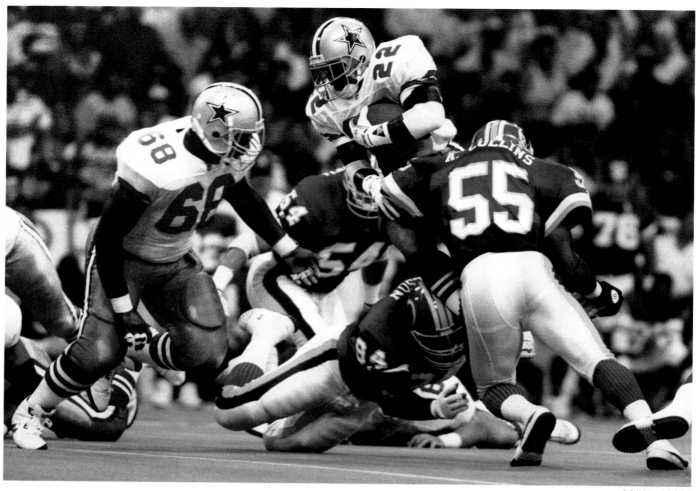

CENTURY MARK Emmitt Smith charges over and through the Redskins' Kurt Gouveia (54, above), Andre Collins (55) and Bobby Wilson on his way to a 139-yard night, then celebrates five-yard touchdown run (below) that put the Cowboys in front, 9-0, in the first quarter. Smith becomes the first rusher to record four consecutive 100-yard games against Washington:

Year	Att.	Yards	Avg.	TD	W-L
1990	17	63	3.7	1	Lost
1990	23	132	5.7	2	Won
1991	11	112	10.2	1	Lost
1991	34	132	3.9	1	Won
1992	26	139	5.3	1	Won

ERICH SCHLEGEL

	1	2	3	4	
WASHINGTON	0	7	0	3	– 10
DALLAS	9	7	7	0	– 23

FIRST QUARTER
Dallas: Safety, Holt blocked punt out of end zone, 3:15.
Dallas: E. Smith 5 run (Elliott kick), 10:54.
SECOND QUARTER
Washington: Clark 30 pass from Rypien (Lohmiller kick), 10:12.
Dallas: Harper 26 pass from Aikman (Elliott kick), 13:58.
THIRD QUARTER
Dallas: Martin 79 punt return (Elliott kick), 8:18.
FOURTH QUARTER
Washington: FG Lohmiller 49, 1:22.
Attendance: 63,538.

TEAM STATS

	Wash.	Dallas
First downs	17	23
Rushes-yards	22-75	35-174
Passing	189	216
Return Yards	59	87
Comp-Att-Int	20-38-0	18-31-2
Sacked-Yards Lost	2-19	0-0
Punts	7-43	4-49
Fumbles-Lost	2-1	0-0
Penalties-Yards	8-80	5-37
Time of Possession	26:47	33:13

RUSHING

Washington: Byner 13-56, Ervins 6-16, Monk 1-8, Rypien 1-0, Sanders 1-(minus 5).
Dallas: E. Smith 26-139, Aikman 8-21, Johnston 1-14.

PASSING

Washington: Rypien 20-38-0-208.
Dallas: Aikman 18-31-2-216.

RECEIVING

Washington: Clark 8-97, Byner 4-31, Sanders 3-20, Monk 2-43, Ervins 2-12, Warren 1-5.
Dallas: Irvin 5-89, Johnston 4-39, Harper 3-59, E.Smith 3-13, Martin 2-12, Novacek 1-4.

MISSED FIELD GOALS

Dallas: Elliott 32.

ERICH SCHLEGEL

ALL HANDS ON DECK Charles Haley (94, top photo), acquired less than two weeks before from San Francisco, pays immediate pass-rush dividends in his Cowboys debut with a crashing sack of Mark Rypien. At left, Alvin Harper (80) slips behind All-Pro cornerback Darrell Green to catch Troy Aikman's picture-perfect pass for a second-quarter touchdown.

EYES FOR DETAIL Troy Aikman throws two touchdown passes to help stake the Cowboys to a 34-0 third-quarter lead...

KEN GEIGER

SEPT. 13, 1992 • GIANTS STADIUM This game was over early but lasted late, anyway.

The Cowboys ran away and hid by streaking to a 34-0 lead early in the third quarter. Then the New York Giants caught them in a dozing posture.

"You never want to think it's over early," Cowboys defensive back Kenneth Gant said, "but in the back of our minds we had to be thinking, 'We got the game wrapped up.'

"It got scary. They could have blocked a punt like us or hit a Hail Mary pass."

As it was, Phil Simms rallied the Giants to within hailing distance of the flustered Cowboys. Simms turned rout into riveting comeback. He delivered drama but still lost the decision, 34-28.

"It's just a relief to get out of New York alive with this one," Coach Jimmy Johnson wheezed. "This tells you how young a team we have. We had a big lead and didn't know how to react."

A wise veteran like Jim Jeffcoat knew enough to be wary.

"That's when a team is most dangerous," he said, referring to the 34-point gap. "They had nothing to lose. Either they make plays or get swamped. As you saw, the Giants made plays."

Jeffcoat's premise lay dormant for months as the work of a mind prone to exaggeration. No team ever lost a 34-point lead. In truth, he made an eerie call of the Buffalo-Houston AFC playoff game.

So the Bills only came from 32 points down. It was Jeffcoat's thought that counted after Buffalo, behind by 35-3, staged the all-time NFL rally Jan. 3 to win in overtime, 41-38.

The Giants flirted with the same feat before the Cowboys restored order. A few minor milestones fell, such as the Cowboys' first victory since 1987 at Giants Stadium and the first block of New York punter Sean Lendeta in five years.

The block co-starred Ken Norton and Robert Williams. Norton applied his nose to the ball; Williams fell on the carom for a touchdown.

"It's almost like they're in a feeding frenzy on the league right now as far as blocking kicks," Giants special teams coach Michael Sweatman said.

Another trend held. A New York writer reminded Emmitt Smith after his 89-yard effort that he had yet to gain 100 yards against the Giants.

"Yes, but we got the win," Smith said. "Which would you rather have, 100 yards or a win? I'll take the win. To hell with 100 yards."

Someone else asked Norton if he felt funny winning a game like this. The inference was of a team that won but got out of town with its pants on fire.

"No, I don't feel funny," said Norton, coming to the point. "I feel 2-0."

GAME 2

| DALLAS | 34 |
| NY GIANTS | 28 |

RANDY GALLOWAY

Sept. 14 column:

As good as they were in building a 34-point mountain, maybe the best thing that happened was Dallas having to desperately defend a molehill of a lead. ...Live, learn and win.

2-0 AND FAR TO GO

The Cowboys' 2-0 start was their 18th in 33 seasons but their first since 1986. The team's final regular-season records in seasons when it won at least its first two games:

Year	Wins at start	Final record
1961	2	4-9-1
1965	2	7-7-0
1966	4	10-3-1
1967	2	9-5-0
1968	6	12-2-0
1969	6	11-2-1
1970	2	10-4-0
1971	2	11-3-0
1972	2	10-4-0
1973	3	10-4-0
1975	4	10-4-0
1976	5	11-3-0
1977	8	12-2-0
1978	2	12-4-0
1979	3	11-5-0
1983	7	12-4-0
1986	2	7-9-0

NAIL-BITER ...but Jimmy Johnson's hair almost ruffles as his team has to sweat out a Giants' comeback. He was less than pleased, despite two personal NFL firsts: a 2-0 start and a victory at Giants Stadium.

MILTON HINNANT

29

DALLAS	17	10	7	0 – 34
NY GIANTS	0	0	14	14 – 28

FIRST QUARTER
Dallas: E. Smith 5 run (Elliott kick), 4:11.
Dallas: R. Williams 3 blocked punt return (Elliott kick), 6:41.
Dallas: FG Elliott 39, 13:37.
SECOND QUARTER
Dallas: FG Elliott 35, 0:57.
Dallas: Novacek 2 pass from Aikman (Elliott kick), 14:28.
THIRD QUARTER
Dallas: Irvin 27 pass from Aikman (Elliott kick), 1:30.
NY Giants: Hampton 5 run (Bahr kick), 5:53.
NY Giants: Bunch 1 pass from Simms (Bahr kick), 14:25.
FOURTH QUARTER
NY Giants: Baker 6 pass from Simms (Bahr kick), 4:35.
NY Giants: Cross 2 pass from Simms (Bahr kick), 8:08.
Attendance: 76,430.

TEAM STATS

	Dallas	NY
First downs	20	22
Rushes-yards	26-98	18-67
Passing	229	264
Return Yards	26	28
Comp-Att-Int	22-35-0	25-42-1
Sacked-Yards Lost	2-9	2-9
Punts	6-42	7-30
Fumbles-Lost	0-0	0-0
Penalties-Yards	7-45	5-43
Time of Possession	31:21	28:39

RUSHING

Dallas: E. Smith 23-89, Aikman 2-8, Johnston 1-1.
NY Giants: Hampton 17-64, Simms 1-3.

PASSING

Dallas: Aikman 22-35-0-238.
NY Giants: Simms 25-42-1-273.

RECEIVING

Dallas: E. Smith 8-55, Novacek 5-33, Irvin 4-73, Martin 2-41, Roberts 1-18, Harper 1-11, Johnston 1-7.
NY Giants: Cross 6-77, McCaffrey 5-82, Hampton 5-36, Calloway 2-23, Bunch 2-7, Meggett 2-(minus 1), J. Smith 1-22, Ingram 1-21, Baker 1-6.

MISSED FIELD GOALS

None.

BANG AND BOFFO Ken Norton (above) smothers the Giants' Sean Landeta for the Cowboys' second punt block in two weeks and the first time since 1987 Landeta had suffered such a fate. Michael Irvin (left) soaks in a mixed reaction after scoring on a 27-yard reception.

SHOULDERING A LOAD

Long before "The Shark" becomes locally famous, Kenneth Gant (29) puts the bite on Rodney Hampton in textbook tackling style. The Cowboys hold Hampton and the Giants to 67 yards rushing.

KEN GEIGER

NO PASSING LANE How better to defend a Phoenix "Hail Mary" than with a former Florida state high-jump champion? Alvin Harper (80, above), normally a receiver on offense, soars over a crowd of Cowboys defenders to knock down a pass intended for an overwhelmed Randall Hill. At right, Larry Brown (24) shows the defensive backs can keep the Cardinals, in this case Ricky Proehl, at arm's length.

SEPT. 20, 1992 • TEXAS STADIUM Michael Irvin erupted. Dave Wannstedt exploded. Amid compliment and curse, the Cowboys kept rolling.

Semi-happy days were here again. It was like the old days. The Cowboys sported a 3-0 record for the first time since 1983.

Old days meant a return of old ways. The Cowboys won and earned lukewarm reviews. At least the defense drew fire from Wannstedt, its coordinator. He blew metallic-blue fumes in the wake of a 31-20 victory over Phoenix marred by Chris Chandler's 383 passing yards.

Irvin blew the Cardinals away. He caught eight passes for a career-best 210 yards. Three went for touchdowns. The longest, on the game's second play, spanned 87 yards with Jay Novacek loping alongside as a blocking screen.

"There's no doubt I'm feeling more in the groove," said Irvin, who didn't sign until Sept. 3 because of a contract dispute. "I needed a big game."

Wannstedt needed cooling off. He didn't feel groovy after seeing a cozy lead melt to narrow margin again. Ahead by 31-13 with 7:58 left, the Cowboys were forced to stop Chandler at their 14-yard line to keep it at 31-20.

Wannstedt huffed about missed tackles, then about defenders being outrebounded by Phoenix receivers, and on to snap at those who dropped two would-be interceptions.

"Stuff like that happens, but it's NOT ACCEPTABLE!" he roared.

Wannstedt sounded distraught enough to accept a spectator for his secondary. So the Cowboys sent him one who had watched the game from owner Jerry Jones' private box.

Safety Thomas Everett, a former Baylor All-America, had arrived via trade from Pittsburgh. He soon would make a difference in pass coverage – and Wannstedt's disposition.

Oddly enough, while Wannstedt railed, Coach Jimmy Johnson nearly raved over the result. Johnson sensed future defensive trends. Adding Charles Haley had improved the pass rush to a persistent, annoying level. Now came the savvy Everett to tighten the secondary.

Johnson reasoned teams passed against the Cowboys because they couldn't run, and run defense is the bedrock key to a championship season. Opponents rack up big aerial numbers but don't win. So what?

"I'm not trying to paint a rosy picture," Johnson said. "I'm not saying I'm 100 percent pleased. But I'm not that concerned."

Even Wannstedt finally relaxed enough to ask: "We *did* win the game, didn't we?"

Ahead beckoned an open date to be filled with hype and hysteria. Next stop for the Cowboys: a stormy Monday night at Veterans Stadium against 3-0 Philadelphia for the NFC East lead.

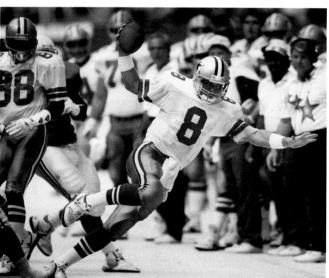

TREADING LIGHTLY Even when he isn't sailing passes, Troy Aikman has his wings out, this time in search of a first down on a scramble.

LOUIS DELUCA

DALLAS 31
PHOENIX 20

TIM COWLISHAW

Sept. 21 game story:
Dallas' 31-20 victory over Phoenix on Sunday made it official. The Cowboys aren't just winning again. Like the old days at Texas Stadium, they are "winning, but…"

FIRST FOR SMITH

Emmitt Smith became the first Cowboy to rush for at least 100 yards in five consecutive home games:

1991	Opponent	Att.	Yards	Avg.	TD
Nov. 28	Pittsburgh	32	109	3.4	1
Dec. 8	New Orleans	27	112	4.1	0
Dec. 22	Atlanta	32	160	5.0	2
1992					
Sept. 7	Washington	26	139	5.3	1
Sept. 20	Phoenix	26	112	4.3	1

EMMITT SMITH

On blocking for teammate Michael Irvin:
"He does so much great blocking for me downfield, I wanted to show him I could help him out, too."

JERRY JONES

"If you had looked at where you'd like to be, no way you could say you'd be 3-0 in this division."

| PHOENIX | 7 | 3 | 3 | 7 – 20 |
| DALLAS | 14 | 7 | 7 | 3 – 31 |

FIRST QUARTER
Dallas: Irvin 87 pass from Aikman (Elliott kick), 1:01.
Phoenix: Hill 34 pass from Chandler (G. Davis kick), 10:13.
Dallas: Irvin 41 pass from Aikman (Elliott kick), 14:40.
SECOND QUARTER
Dallas: E. Smith 1 run (Elliott kick), 11:30.
Phoenix: FG G. Davis 22, 13:37.
THIRD QUARTER
Dallas: Irvin 4 pass from Aikman (Elliott kick), 7:32.
Phoenix: FG G. Davis 42, 10:51.
FOURTH QUARTER
Dallas: FG Elliott 29, 7:02.
Phoenix: Brown 1 run (G. Davis kick), 10:13.
Attendance: 62,575.

TEAM STATS

	Phoenix	Dallas
First downs	24	21
Rushes-yards	17-67	38-150
Passing	371	263
Return Yards	35	0
Comp-Att-Int	28-43-0	14-21-0
Sacked-Yards Lost	2-12	0-0
Punts	2-52	3-51
Fumbles-Lost	2-2	0-0
Penalties-Yards	6-37	3-14
Time of Possession	25:59	34:01

RUSHING

Phoenix: Brown 12-31, Bailey 2-22, Chandler 2-12, Centers 1-2.
Dallas: E. Smith 26-112, Richards 7-32, Aikman 1-8, Johnston 3-7, Irvin 1-(minus 9).

PASSING

Phoenix: Chandler 28-43-0-383.
Dallas: Aikman 14-21-0-263.

RECEIVING

Phoenix: Centers 7-64, Jones 5-78, Proehl 4-51, Rolle 4-19, Bailey 3-53, Hill 2-74, Brown 2-31, Johnson 1-13.
Dallas: Irvin 8-210, Novacek 3-28, Harper 1-14, Martin 1-7, Richards 1-4.

MISSED FIELD GOALS

None.

IT'S CATCHING Michael Irvin has a day to remember against the Cardinals, wrapping himself around eight receptions for a career-high 210 yards and three touchdowns. He beats Lorenzo Lynch (29, right) for one catch and, on the facing page, is all alone to make an overhead grab in the flat.

DAVID PELLERIN

LOUIS DELUCA

MY BALL Tony Casillas (75, above) makes like a fullback, ridden to the turf by Lance Smith, after recovering Chris Chandler's third-quarter fumble. Casillas' play sets up the Cowboys for Troy Aikman's four-yard touchdown pass to Michael Irvin.

STEVE HAMM

HARD NIGHT'S WORK Seth Joyner's bulldog tackle on Jay Novacek (84) forces an incomplete pass in the first quarter against Philadelphia. Below, Michael Irvin's headlong dive between the Eagles' Otis Smith (30) and Mark McMillian can't prevent another pass from hitting the turf.

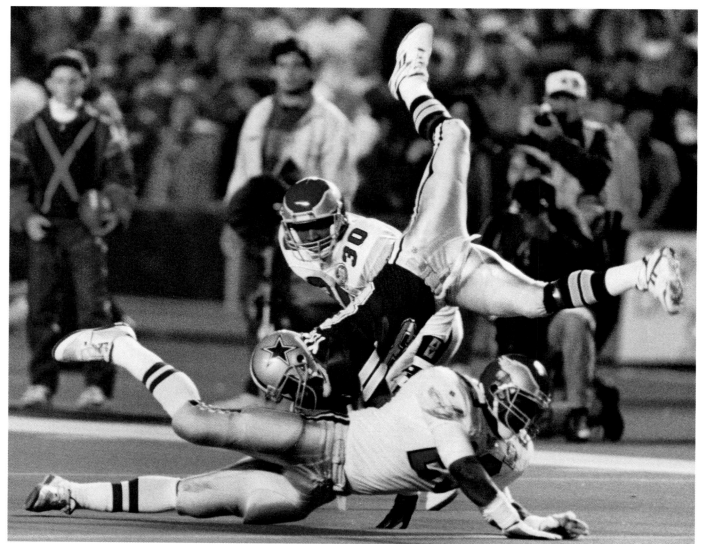

OCT. 5, 1992 • VETERANS STADIUM The Cowboys and Philadelphia Eagles duked it out in a game longer than The Creation to produce and almost as widely advertised. And from the Cowboys' viewpoint, at least, not worth a two-week wait to play.

They were knocked out, 31-7.

A boisterous Veterans Stadium crowd of 66,572 howled with delight and derision. Eagles fans even spent less time than usual fighting each other.

By thrusting aside the Cowboys so forcefully, the 4-0 Eagles assumed a one-game lead in the NFC East. Philadelphia and Miami were the NFL's remaining unbeatens, and the Eagles appeared the league's dominant team.

Appearances proved deceiving. Within a mere two weeks, the Cowboys would hold a one-game lead over the Eagles.

Philadelphia, meanwhile, basked in the pay-back aspects of its romp. On the same site 10 months earlier, the Cowboys had eliminated the Eagles from playoff contention with a 25-13 victory. Then there was the irony of a ghost returning to haunt the Cowboys.

Herschel Walker played against his former team for the first time since his 1989 trade to the Minnesota Vikings for a Spanish Armada of players and draft choices. He played a prominent role, too. Walker rushed for 86 yards, caught three passes and scored on runs of nine and 16 yards.

The Cowboys, by comparison, ran and passed themselves into defeat. They confirmed coach Jimmy Johnson's worst pre-game fears.

"The biggest thing against Philadelphia is to avoid negative plays," Johnson had warned. "They make some plays on defense, and they get into a feeding frenzy. You have to avoid that."

The Cowboys didn't. The Eagles feasted on three interceptions and one fumble. They cashed three turnovers into 21 points and drove no farther than 52 yards to score. A 10-7 Philadelphia halftime lead mushroomed out of control down the stretch.

"Turnovers killed us…fumbles, interceptions and whatever else took place out there," quarterback Troy Aikman said.

ERICH SCHLEGEL

Someone mentioned to veteran safety-linebacker Bill Bates that the Eagles looked like the best of the rest. Bates offered a telling reply.

"Now we'll see how they respond to that challenge," he said.

With 12 games to play, Bates already had diagnosed the fleeting nature of a single result. What mattered now was how the Cowboys reacted to galling defeat and the Eagles to satisfying victory.

And it was here, at the apex of Philadelphia's season, that the NFC East rivals began to go their separate ways. The Cowboys were poised for a 5-1 run, while the Eagles were about to begin a 2-4 swoon.

MICHAEL IRVIN "It's the fourth game of the season. It's not the championship game. It's not a playoff game. You don't have to go home. The first thing you do after you lose like this? You jump back in the fight."

PHILADELPHIA 31
DALLAS 7

RANDY GALLOWAY
Oct. 6 column:
…this Monday night test against a hostile team in hostile territory before a massive TV audience was certainly viewed as a measuring stick for Dallas. Against the Eagles, however, only the short end of the stick was showing when this thing was over.

TIM COWLISHAW
Oct. 6 game story:
Where Randall Cunningham was cool in the pocket, Troy Aikman was just cold. At least this time he wasn't knocked cold.

TONY CASILLAS
"Sure, there was a lot of hype. But we'll be back. The season is only a few weeks old."

BREASTSTROKE Seth Joyner (59) has an arm up on Emmitt Smith as they scramble after Smith's fumble, but Michael Irvin would beat both of them to the loose ball.

AIKMAN VS. EAGLES Jimmy Johnson and Troy Aikman have a long night trying to figure out something that would work against the tough Eagles defense. Aikman was intercepted three times, or one more than in the first three games combined. It continued his career-long trend of subpar outings against Philadelphia:

Year	Cmp.	Att.	Yards	TD	Int.	Sacks
1989	17	21	54	0	3	1
	17	30	152	1	0	5
1990	22	41	233	1	1	2
	0	1	0	0	0	1
1991	11	25	112	0	3	11
1992	19	38	231	1	3	4

ERICH SCHLEGEL

	DALLAS	PHILADELPHIA
	7 0 0 0 – 7	10 0 7 14 – 31

FIRST QUARTER
Philadelphia: Cunningham 2 run (Ruzek kick), 3:25.
Dallas: Martin 7 pass from Aikman (Elliott kick), 7:05.
Philadelphia: FG Ruzek 40, 13:26.
THIRD QUARTER
Philadelphia: Walker 9 run (Ruzek kick), 9:59.
FOURTH QUARTER
Philadelphia: Walker 16 run (Ruzek kick), 2:20.
Philadelphia: Byars 12 run (Ruzek kick), 11:56.

Attendance: 66,572.

TEAM STATS

	Dallas	Phil.
First downs	17	21
Rushes-yards	22-80	36-160
Passing	231	106
Return Yards	19	55
Comp-Att-Int	19-38-3	11-19-1
Sacked-Yards Lost	4-25	2-18
Punts	4-41	4-53
Fumbles-Lost	1-1	1-0
Penalties-Yards	9-58	4-30
Time of Possession	29:15	30:45

RUSHING
Dallas: E. Smith 19-67, Agee 2-11, Johnston 1-2.
Philadelphia: Walker 19-86, Cunningham 7-43, Byars 8-25, Sherman 2-6.

PASSING
Dallas: Aikman 19-38-3-256.
Philadelphia: Cunningham 11-19-1-124.

RECEIVING
Dallas: Novacek 6-61, Irvin 4-105, Martin 3-31, E. Smith 2-5, Harper 1-42, Gesek 1-4, Roberts 1-4, Agee 1-4.
Philadelphia: Barnett 5-76, Walker 3-14, Byars 1-14, Williams 1-13, Beach 1-7.

MISSED FIELD GOALS
Dallas: Elliott 48.

LOUIS DELUCA

FASTER ON THE DRAW John Booty (42, above) leaves Kelvin Martin hanging as he snatches away the Eagles' first interception and then returns it 22 yards to set up their first touchdown. At left, Cowboys safety James Washington (37) has the inside track to a fumble by Heath Sherman, but neither Washington nor teammate Vinson Smith (57) can get to it before the Eagles retain possession.

RUN DEFENSE Rookie middle line-backer Robert Jones (above), part of a defense that holds Seattle to a Cowboys-record 62 yards, fights off John L. Williams' stiff-arm attempt for a tackle. At right, Seahawks safety Eugene Robinson (41) takes the low road to cut down Emmitt Smith.

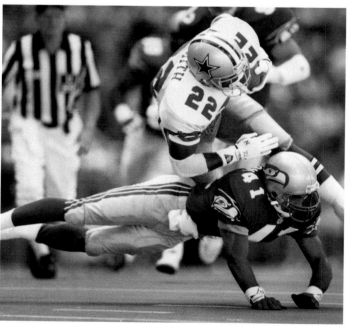

OCT. 11, 1992 • TEXAS STADIUM The Seattle Seahawks will recall their visit as a pointless exercise. The Cowboys blanked them, 27-0.

Multiple dividends evolved as the Cowboys bounced back with vigor from their 31-7 loss at Philadelphia. If not foremost, the most obvious was the team's first regular-season shutout since 1978.

The defense added other scalps. It set a club record by allowing only 62 yards, one fewer than the previous low in 1965 against Green Bay. Seven sacks, two fumble recoveries and Ray Horton's 15-yard interception return for a touchdown were other highlight-film entries.

As a bonus, Kansas City beat Philadelphia, 24-17, an outcome coach Jimmy Johnson watched on an interview-room television before offering his post-game capsules. The Cowboys now shared the NFC East lead with the Eagles at 4-1.

The lone somber note was a knee injury to special teams star Bill Bates. His season ended early.

Depleted by injury and opting to start immobile 6-foot-8 rookie Dan McGwire at quarterback, Seattle went nowhere. The Seahawks gained eight yards in the last three quarters.

"It was a track meet to see who could get back there first," said end Jim Jeffcoat, who had two sacks.

Rookie middle linebacker Robert Jones supplied the flavor of the chase. He blitzed free in the third quarter to disable McGwire.

"I had a clear shot," he said. "It was as if the Red Sea parted."

Intent to complete a whitewash, the Cowboys took no prisoners. Puny as the Seahawks were on offense, Tony Casillas found considerable merit in snuffing them anyway.

"People are going to say, 'It was only Seattle,' but I don't care who you play," he said. "You have that kind of performance, and you deserve some respect."

The Cowboys were earning respect from NFL experts. Bill Parcells, the former New York Giants coach turned NBC Sports analyst, cast an approving eye on their progress.

"The situation in Dallas is not unlike the one I took over," he said. "We went to the play-offs twice and then won the Super Bowl. It's interesting to watch teams take certain steps. The Cowboys appear to be taking the right ones."

The most improbable steps against Seattle belonged to guard John Gesek. He caught safety Eugene Robinson at the end of a 49-yard runback of a tipped interception. Gesek struggled to explain how his battered knees won that race.

"Say I had an adrenaline burst. How's that?" he said with a smile.

Gesek unknowingly had described the Cowboys as a whole. A five-game winning streak was in progress.

GAME 5

DALLAS 27
SEATTLE 0

SHUT DOWN

The Cowboys' defense held Seattle to 62 yards, a club record for fewest allowed in a game. The top three:

Date	Opponent	Yards
Oct. 11, 1992	Seattle	62
Oct. 24, 1965	Green Bay	63
Nov. 6, 1966	Philadelphia	80

KENNY GANT

On replacing Ray Horton as a starting safety:

"I'm sure they (the coaches) have their reasons for what they did. I'm just glad to get an opportunity to play."

KEN NORTON

"Until we play Philly again, we're just going to beat up on everybody else."

COWBOYS' SHUTOUTS

The 27-0 victory over Seattle was the Cowboys' 13th shutout:

Date	Opponent	Score
Oct. 8, 1961	Minnesota	28-0
Oct. 11, 1970	Atlanta	13-0
Dec. 6, 1970	Washington	34-0
Dec. 26, 1970	Detroit*	5-0
Nov. 21, 1971	Washington	13-0
Oct. 15, 1972	Baltimore	21-0
Sept. 15, 1974	Atlanta	24-0
Nov. 24, 1974	Houston	10-0
Oct. 30, 1977	Detroit	37-0
Sept. 4, 1978	Baltimore	38-0
Jan. 7, 1979	LA Rams*	28-0
Jan. 2, 1981	Tampa Bay*	38-0
Oct. 11, 1992	Seattle	27-0

* Playoff game

THOUGHTFUL Jimmy Johnson, watching his team demolish Seattle, waited until Kansas City had beaten Philadelphia before giving reporters his post-game analysis. The Chiefs' victory helped the Cowboys regain a share of the NFC East lead.

DAVID PELLERIN

41

NO QUARTER GIVEN Seattle's offense has no chance against the Cowboys' smothering defense. Tony Tolbert (92, above) drags down Dan McGwire with one of the Cowboys' seven sacks, and linemates Leon Lett (78, right) and Jimmie Jones (97) combine to punish McGwire again. Rookie cornerback Kevin Smith (26, middle right) gives McGwire nowhere to throw when he does get one off, and Russell Maryland (67, far right) and Robert Jones team up to finish McGwire's day with another crushing sack.

KEN GEIGER

DONNA BAGBY

CAROLYN HERTER

	Seattle	Dallas
SEATTLE	0 0 0 0	– 0
DALLAS	7 13 7 0	– 27

FIRST QUARTER
Dallas: E. Smith 2 run (Elliott kick), 3:43.
SECOND QUARTER
Dallas: E. Smith 1 run (Elliott kick), 5:36.
Dallas: FG Elliott 31, 8:12.
Dallas: FG Elliott 51, 13:09.
THIRD QUARTER
Dallas: Horton 15 interception return (Elliott kick), 10:16.
Attendance: 62,311.

TEAM STATS

	Seattle	Dallas
First downs	6	16
Rushes-yards	22-38	30-116
Passing	24	197
Return Yards	49	26
Comp-Att-Int	8-19-1	17-28-2
Sacked-Yards Lost	7-55	1-3
Punts	8-49	5-46
Fumbles-Lost	3-2	0-0
Penalties-Yards	7-40	3-15
Time of Possession	26:44	33:16

RUSHING

Seattle: Warren 7-14, Mayes 4-12, J.L. Williams 8-10, McGwire 2-2, Gelbaugh 1-0.
Dallas: E. Smith 22-78, Aikman 1-19, Agee 3-10, Johnston 4-9.

PASSING

Seattle: McGwire 5-9-0-46, Gelbaugh 3-10-1-33.
Dallas: Aikman 15-23-2-173, Beuerlein 2-5-0-27.

RECEIVING

Seattle: R. Thomas 3-28, J.L. Williams 3-24, Daniels 1-15, D. Thomas 1-12.
Dallas: Irvin 6-113, Novacek 5-22, Martin 4-45, Harper 2-20.

MISSED FIELD GOALS

Seattle: Kasay 40.
Dallas: Elliott 42.

KEN GEIGER

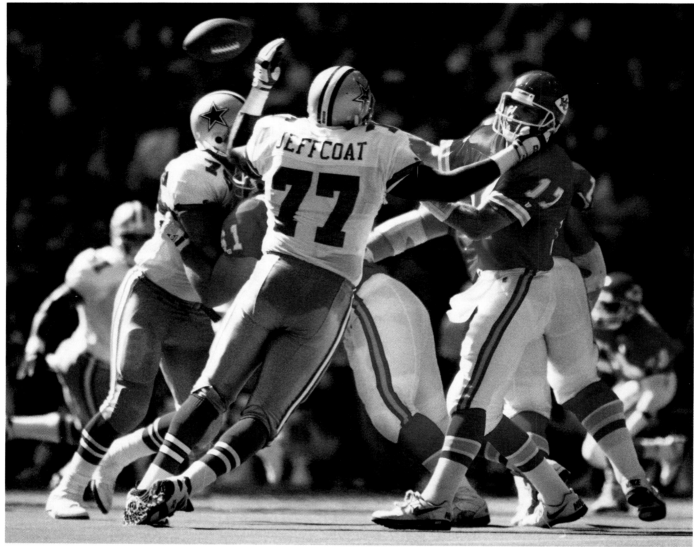

HEAVY TRAFFIC The Cowboys sack the Chiefs' Dave Krieg (17) three times, and Jim Jeffcoat (77) narrowly misses another as he bats down Krieg's pass. One week after holding Seattle to a record-low 62 yards, the Cowboys' defense, on its way to a No. 1 league ranking, limits Krieg and the Chiefs to 230 yards.

CATCHING ON Emmitt Smith (22) spectates as Jay Novacek (84) makes one of his five receptions against Kansas City. On pages 46-47 (photo by Louis DeLuca), Smith puts himself in the foreground when he runs the ball, as he makes Charles Mincy miss.

OCT. 18, 1992 • TEXAS STADIUM Self-abused by a season-high 11 penalties, the Cowboys demonstrated the value of winning ugly rather than losing pretty.

The Cowboys beat Kansas City, 17-10, to the squirming pleasure of 64,115 fans. Coupled with a 16-12 Washington victory over Philadelphia, the Cowboys found themselves alone atop the NFC East with a 6-1 record.

They were there to stay. Having gained solo entry to the penthouse, the Cowboys pulled up the ladder behind them and posted a sign: "Occupied. No Vacancy. Loitering Also Prohibited."

There were subtle achievements to savor alongside the Cowboys' 10th consecutive home victory. One belonged to their coach, who crossed an invisible barrier.

GAME 6

At this moment, for the first time since he replaced Tom Landry in 1989, Jimmy Johnson had his team alone at the division pinnacle. Johnson so liked the view, he filed for squatter's rights.

Another asterisk attached to Emmitt Smith, 23, after he gained 95 yards and increased his career rushing total to 3,081. Smith became the youngest back in NFL history to surpass the 3,000-yard mark.

Powerful but ponderous, Kansas City died hard. The Chiefs were within 22 yards of a tying touchdown when Ray Horton intercepted Dave Krieg's pass with 3:27 left. A week earlier, Horton had scored on a pick against Seattle.

Irony and a thin sheen of anger cloaked Horton's big plays since he came off the bench to make them. A starter previously, he had lost his first-team job.

"I believe in handling things with class and dignity, even though I felt like a leper and outcast," he said.

Horton's presence as game-saving figure illustrated an emerging factor about the Cowboys' roster. It was deep in quality reserves. Offensive tackle Alan Veingrad provided another example.

Veingrad subbed for Mark Tuinei, out with a strained back. Playing head-up against Kansas City sack-master Derrick Thomas, Veingrad won a game ball for distinguished service.

No one on offense had a soft day at the office. As center Mark Stepnoski put it, tangling with the Chiefs was "like sumo wrestling for three hours."

Nor could the defense rest. When the penalty-infested mess unraveled, stingy defense proved the difference.

"This defense is coming around," tackle Tony Casillas said. It was coming on and coming up. The defense would keep rising until it ranked No. 1 in the NFL.

HOLD ON Michael Irvin turns into a defender, stopping rookie Dale Carter after an interception. Irvin caught six passes for 84 yards.

LOUIS DELUCA

| DALLAS | 17 |
| KANSAS CITY | 10 |

KANSAS CITY	3	7	0	0 –	10
DALLAS	7	7	3	0 –	17

FIRST QUARTER
Kansas City: FG Lowery 32, 8:30.
Dallas: Johnston 2 pass from Aikman (Elliott kick), 13:57.
SECOND QUARTER
Dallas: E. Smith 2 run (Elliott kick), 3:55.
Kansas City: Word 2 run (Lowery kick), 13:03.
THIRD QUARTER
Dallas: FG Elliott 39, 7:36.
Attendance: 64,115.

TEAM STATS

	KC	Dallas
First downs	18	17
Rushes-yards	25-91	24-95
Passing	139	183
Return Yards	57	50
Comp-Att-Int	16-31-1	21-29-2
Sacked-Yards Lost	3-31	1-9
Punts	6-39	4-46
Fumbles-Lost	1-0	0-0
Penalties-Yards	5-54	11-74
Time of Possession	30:47	29:13

RUSHING

Kansas City: Word 13-46, Williams 6-28, Okoye 5-17, Krieg 1-0.
Dallas: E. Smith 24-95.

PASSING

Kansas City: Krieg 16-31-1-170.
Dallas: Aikman 21-29-2-192.

RECEIVING

Kansas City: Davis 6-100, McNair 3-16, F.Jones 2-24, Birden 1-10, Harry 1-7, Hayes 1-6, Word 1-5, Anders 1-2.
Dallas: Irvin 6-84, Novacek 5-36, Johnston 5-29, E. Smith 4-36, Agee 1-8.

MISSED FIELD GOALS

Dallas: Elliott 51.

WILLIAM SNYDER

KEVIN B. BLACKISTONE

Oct. 26 column:

Instead, (Los Angeles Raiders owner Al) Davis got a visitor's crowd spurred by the resurgent America's Team. And it was his counterpart from Texas who celebrated the noise. (The Cowboys' fans) stood and chanted their favorite team's name when Aikman scored the game-breaking touchdown (above). ...They did so again when Emmitt Smith salted the contest away, 28-13. Smith even took a 200-meter victory walk before them...

VICTORY SALUTE Michael Irvin responds to the thousands of Cowboys fans who filled the Los Angeles Memorial Coliseum. The crowd of 91,505 is the largest in Cowboys history.

WILLIAM SNYDER

OCT. 25, 1992 • LOS ANGELES MEMORIAL COLISEUM An egocentric baseball manager once told his team, "Stay close for eight innings, and then I'll think of something." Jimmy Johnson had a shorter version of the same theory in mind before facing the Los Angeles Raiders.

Stay close early, and we'll wear them down late, Johnson advised during a pre-game lecture.

"I told the team the Raiders would be at their very best in the first quarter," he said. "I also said that if we can hang in there and stay even in the first quarter, we can win. And that's what we did."

The Cowboys won, 28-13, by breaking away to score 21 unanswered points in the second half. And by breaking loose Emmitt Smith for 152 yards and three touchdowns.

GAME 7

| DALLAS | 28 |
| LA RAIDERS | 13 |

"I think it's our youth, our conditioning and strength. It all showed up in the second half," defensive coordinator Dave Wannstedt said.

Whatever it was about the Cowboys, 91,505 fans jammed the Los Angeles Coliseum to witness. It was the largest regular-season crowd in Cowboys history, besting the 85,850 at Cleveland in 1969.

"Wherever we go, you see big crowds," safety James Washington said. "I think people like the Cowboys."

This immense crowd did, openly cheering for the Cowboys as if they were the home team. And in truth, they had returned to near their former training base in Thousand Oaks, Calif.

There was much to cheer as the Cowboys improved to 6-1 with their third consecutive victory. Smith's spree, keyed by scoring runs of six, four and 26 yards, was standing-O stuff.

Smith drew even more attention standing still. He caused a gasp by leaving the field limping in the third quarter with the Cowboys behind, 13-7.

"Emmitt was standing by my side when he said, 'Coach, I'm ready to go back in,'" Johnson said. "Well, if Emmitt is ready to go, I'm ready to go with him."

Smith re-entered the lineup as the game changed on a 52-yard pass from Troy Aikman to Alvin Harper. Smith's four-yard touchdown run established a 14-13 lead the Cowboys methodically increased.

It was a special moment for Harper, fated to play in the flamboyant shadow of sidekick Michael Irvin.

"I was just thinking what a great opportunity it was for me to make the big play and show everybody I could do it," Harper said. "It was something I needed, to make a big play when they call my number and get myself some more confidence."

As the season wore on, Harper would be asked to make more big plays. The biggest was yet to come, and that one would ensure the Cowboys a Super Bowl berth.

ALVIN HARPER

On his team-leading four catches for 79 yards:

"…they knew they'd have to come to me at some point. They knew there would be a time when somebody took Michael (Irvin) away. They just threw to the open man, and that was me."

JERRY JONES

"Maybe we've gotten used to playing in Los Angeles. We'll see."

JIM JEFFCOAT

"We want to show people on the West Coast and East Coast that the Cowboys come to play."

LOUIS DELUCA

SMITH ON GRASS He's no ordinary back on artificial turf, but Emmitt Smith, shown here charging through the Raiders' defense, becomes an extraordinary back on natural turf. His last six games on grass fields:

Year	Opponent	Att.	Yds.	TD	Result
'91	Cleveland	32	112	0	W, 26-14
'91	Phoenix	23	182	2	W, 17-9
'91	Green Bay	32	122	0	W, 20-17
'91	Washington	34	132	1	W, 24-21
'91	Chicago	26	105	1	W, 17-13
'92	LA Raiders	29	152	3	W, 28-13

DALLAS	7	0	7	14 – 28
LA RAIDERS	6	0	7	0 – 13

FIRST QUARTER
LA Raiders: Allen 1 run (pass failed), 4:40.
Dallas: E. Smith 6 run (Elliott kick), 13:28.
THIRD QUARTER
LA Raiders: Gault 31 pass from Marinovich (Jaeger kick), 4:18.
Dallas: E. Smith 4 run (Elliott kick), 7:23.
FOURTH QUARTER
Dallas: Aikman 3 run (Elliott kick), 4:54.
Dallas: E. Smith 26 run (Elliott kick), 11:34.
Attendance: 91,505.

TEAM STATS

	Dallas	LA
First downs	23	12
Rushes-yards	39-162	20-71
Passing	207	94
Return Yards	47	54
Comp-Att-Int	16-25-0	8-26-0
Sacked-Yards Lost	5-27	3-23
Punts	5-37	6-45
Fumbles-Lost	2-0	2-1
Penalties-Yards	7-56	5-28
Time of Possession	37:17	22:43

RUSHING
Dallas: E. Smith 29-152, Aikman 8-4, Johnston 1-4, Richards 1-2.
LA Raiders: Dickerson 8-42, Allen 3-9, S. Smith 4-7, Schroeder 2-5, N.Bell 2-4, Marinovich 1-4.

PASSING
Dallas: Aikman 16-25-0-234.
LA Raiders: Marinovich 8-23-0-117, Schroeder 0-3-0-0.

RECEIVING
Dallas: Harper 4-79, Novacek 3-60, Irvin 3-54, E. Smith 3-15, Johnston 2-11, Martin 1-15.
LA Raiders: T. Brown 2-28, S.Smith 2-13, Gault 1-31, E. Horton 1-26, Glover 1-10, Fernandez 1-9.

MISSED FIELD GOALS
Dallas: Elliott 48.

ANOTHER PRIZE Leon Lett holds his trophy aloft after making a fumble recovery against the Raiders. Los Angeles manages only 165 yards and 12 first downs.

WILLIAM SNYDER

IN THEIR GRASP Larry Brown (24, above) tries to drag down holder Jeff Gossett after the Raiders botch an extra-point attempt. Gossett would break free but throw an incomplete pass. At left, Ray Horton and Tony Tolbert (92) ride Eric Dickerson to the turf, as the Cowboys hold the former All-Pro to 42 yards.

NOV. 1, 1992 • TEXAS STADIUM A mid-season rematch between the Cowboys and Philadelphia Eagles settled the issue of who belonged where in the NFC East. A 20-10 victory at rowdy Texas Stadium confirmed the 7-1 Cowboys belonged where they were – in first place.

Beating the Eagles avenged an earlier 31-7 defeat at Philadelphia and opened a two-game lead on a fading cast of division rivals. It also extended the Cowboys winning streaks to 11 at home and four overall.

"Our 7-1 record is about as far away as you can get from a couple of years ago," said center Mark Stepnoski, a survivor of that 1989 season when the Cowboys won all but 15 of 16 games.

GAME 8

This was a game of firsts and lasts. As in:

■ The first time Troy Aikman beat the Eagles in seven tries.

■ The first time Eagles quarterback Randall Cunningham lost to the Cowboys in nine games.

■ The first time in 54 games a runner (Emmitt Smith with 163 yards) hit the Eagles for 100 yards rushing.

■ The first time the Cowboys beat Philadelphia at home in a non-strike game since 1985.

But not the last time, as future playoff events would dictate.

"It was a big step for us and a big win for me and our team," Aikman said. "But it's only important if we continue to take care of business one game at a time."

In the absence of NFL doubleheaders, this was easily done. Much easier than the task young tackle Erik Williams handled with veteran aplomb. Williams went head-to-head against premier pass rusher Reggie White and won the battle hands down.

Depth again was on display for the Cowboys. Kelvin Martin, the No. 3 wide receiver, fled the bench to lead all receivers with seven catches for 83 yards and one touchdown.

Surprise became another factor. Daryl Johnston, the pulling guard who plays fullback, slipped free to catch a 14-yard touchdown pass.

The brightest stars shined on defense, which had climbed to the NFL's No. 1 ranking. Cunningham was so useless (13 yards passing), coach Rich Kotite replaced him with Jim McMahon.

Herschel Walker made less impact in his return engagement, gaining 44 hard yards. In fact, the Cowboys began to dominate after a late third-quarter engagement at their one-yard line. The Eagles owned a first down at that spot but were held to a field goal that tied the score, 10-10.

"We just lined up with each man and beat him," defensive tackle Tony Casillas said. "We felt like we owed them one."

JOHN F. RHODES

HIGH TIME Daryl Johnston (48), whose primary value is as Emmitt Smith's lead blocker, shows his acrobatic side by sailing over Philadelphia's John Booty to complete a 14-yard touchdown reception. Johnston's fourth-quarter score, as at least one fan (right) puts it, cooks the Eagles' chances.

| DALLAS | 20 |
| PHILADELPHIA | 10 |

RANDY GALLOWAY

Nov. 2 column:
Game on the line at Texas Stadium, and (Emmitt) Smith was blowing through holes, around tacklers, off tacklers. Open wide, Philly. The ball is being shoved down your eight-man-front throat. ...The Cowboys won a game against their biggest headache in the league and also proved an interesting point. They can and will slam-dance against the feared Eagles defense.

THOMAS EVERETT

"Talent-wise, we probably have one of the top two or three teams in the league. We're hitting now."

LIN ELLIOTT

On missing field goals from 42 and 38 yards:
"Regardless of what happens, I feel I'm a good kicker. What I'm going through right now will thicken my skin a little bit."

TROY AIKMAN

On his first victory against Philadelphia:
"Yeah, I'll put it into perspective. It's no more important than last week's game... and it's no more important than next week's game..."

INS AND OUTS Emmitt Smith plows through the Eagles' vaunted defense on one of his 30 carries for 163 yards, the first 100-yard rushing day against Philadelphia in three years. At right, Herschel Walker returns to Texas Stadium for the first time since his 1989 trade to limited success. The Cowboys, in the turning point of the second half, stop him twice at the goal line, forcing a field goal. Walker appears to shove the ball over the line, but officials rule his forward progress had been stopped.

LOUIS DELUCA

PHILADELPHIA	0 0 10 0 – 10
DALLAS	0 3 7 10 – 20

SECOND QUARTER
Dallas: FG Elliott 35, 14:39.
THIRD QUARTER
Philadelphia: Walker 2 run (Ruzek kick), 4:36.
Dallas: Martin 22 pass from Aikman (Elliott kick), 7:27.
Philadelphia: FG Ruzek 18, 13:05.
FOURTH QUARTER
Dallas: FG Elliott 48, :05.
Dallas: Johnston 14 pass from Aikman (Elliott kick), 7:21.
Attendance: 65,012.

TEAM STATS

	Phil.	Dallas
First downs	9	22
Rushes-yards	21-73	35-175
Passing	117	214
Return Yards	52	61
Comp-Att-Int	13-27-2	19-33-1
Sacked-Yards Lost	2-18	1-0
Punts	8-46	5-34
Fumbles-Lost	0-0	1-1
Penalties-Yards	5-31	5-28
Time of Possession	24:40	35:20

RUSHING

Philadelphia: Walker 16-44, McMahon 2-21, Byars 2-5, Cunningham 1-3.
Dallas: E. Smith 30-163, Aikman 4-11, Johnston 1-1.

PASSING

Philadelphia: McMahon 10-19-1-122, Cunningham 3-8-1-13.
Dallas: Aikman 19-33-1-214.

RECEIVING

Philadelphia: Byars 6-37, Williams 2-54, Walker 2-5, Barnett 1-15, Green 1-13, Sikahema 1-11.
Dallas: Martin 7-83, Johnston 4-46, Novacek 4-38, Irvin 2-29, E. Smith 1-9, Harper 1-9.

MISSED FIELD GOALS

Dallas: Elliott 42, 38.

LOUIS DELUCA

BALANCED AND BOUNCED Jay Novacek (84, above) shows his fine hands – or hand, in this case – in cradling one his four receptions against the Eagles. Charles Haley (94, left) and the Cowboys defense make life so miserable for Randall Cunningham that he is pulled from the game.

UP AND OVER A clearing block by John Gesek (63) helps Emmitt Smith slice past the Lions' Chris Spielman (54) for one of his three touchdowns at the Silverdome. Smith ties a club record with his 12th rushing score of the season.

NOV. 8, 1992 • PONTIAC SILVERDOME The Cowboys continued to avenge old scores and heal festering wounds. Naturally, they also continued to win.

The site was almost as novel as the sound of their fifth consecutive victory. A hushed sellout crowd of 74,816 ringed the Silverdome as the 8-1 Cowboys hammered the Detroit Lions, 37-3.

"This was just another game we had to win," defensive coordinator Dave Wannstedt said. "But there was a little extra baggage on this one."

Wannstedt referred to a return to the scene of twin crimes during the 1991 season. The Cowboys were found guilty of criminal negligence and impersonating a playoff team at the Silverdome.

GAME 9

DALLAS	37
DETROIT	3

In doing so, they lost to the Lions by scores of 34-10 and 38-6.

All that got lost this time was Jimmy Johnson's temper. Michael Irvin missed the team flight to Detroit, drew a $1,000 fine and game-long frown from his coach, despite catching five passes for 114 yards.

"Michael is one of my favorites," Johnson said. "I guess it cuts deeper when one of your favorites doesn't do what you want."

Everyone else played above reproach. That included troubled rookie kicker Lin Elliott, who hit field goals from 25, 42 and 30 yards. The week before, against the Eagles, he missed kicks of 42 and 38 yards and heard boos from unhappy fans at home.

"It's pretty ironic, going from the worst groove of your career to a good groove in a matter of six or seven kicks," Elliott marveled. "It feels good to be back on track."

The defense, meanwhile, buried a worrisome bone. Run-and-Shoot attacks had given the Cowboys fits. Not this time. The Lions gained only 77 yards passing, and their quarterbacks twice were intercepted by safety Thomas Everett.

"When we played them last year, our game plan centered more on stopping Barry Sanders," defensive end Tony Tolbert said. "This time, we were thinking pass and reacting to the run. We were on the quarterback all day long, I know that."

Said Charles Haley of a defense already ranked No. 1 in the league: "I think we're getting better week to week. That's a great feeling for a defense, to keep a team out of the end zone."

Emmitt Smith spent much of his day there. He scored three times to tie a club record of 12 rushing touchdowns in a season. Smith had seven games to break that mark and another for most touchdowns (16) in a season.

"An excellent football team in every phase," Lions coach Wayne Fontes said of the Cowboys, who were riding high. And riding for a fall.

POOR POSITIONS

The Cowboys used turnovers and special-teams play to establish a field-position advantage. The Lions' 11 offensive possessions:

Start	Plays	Yards	Result
Detroit 32	1	10	Fumble
Detroit 1	7	64	Interception
Detroit 16	3	-4	Punt
Detroit 7	3	3	Punt
Detroit 22	9	60	Field goal
Detroit 8	3	-3	Punt
Detroit 38	4	13	Interception
Detroit 38	3	1	Punt
Detroit 22	4	18	Interception
Detroit 20	4	18	Punt
Detroit 30	1	1	End of game

MICHAEL IRVIN

On missing the team plane to Detroit:

"I'm not going to give you an explanation. I don't give my wife an explanation. Don't bug me. Let it go."

TROY AIKMAN

After Coach Jimmy Johnson's pre-game speech on "focus":

"I'm just glad we won, or we'd be hearing about it every minute the rest of the season."

HE PASSES, TOO
Issiac Holt (30) can't elude a wristband fired at his back by Emmitt Smith. Holt earned the playful rebuke by swiping Smith's cap.

LOUIS DELUCA

DALLAS	14	6	14	3 – 37
DETROIT	0	3	0	0 – 3

FIRST QUARTER
Dallas: E. Smith 7 run (Elliott kick), 12:22.
Dallas: E. Smith 1 run (Elliott kick), 14:51.
SECOND QUARTER
Detroit: FG Hanson 36, 5:48.
Dallas: FG Elliott 25, 13:34.
Dallas: FG Elliott 42, 14:57.
THIRD QUARTER
Dallas: E. Smith 1 run (Elliott kick), 2:33.
Dallas: Irvin 15 pass from Aikman (Elliott kick), 14:47.
FOURTH QUARTER
Dallas: FG Elliott 30, 14:40.
Attendance: 74,816.

TEAM STATS

	Dallas	Detroit
First downs	26	10
Rushes-yards	37-158	22-124
Passing	240	77
Return Yards	50	21
Comp-Att-Int	18-27-1	9-17-3
Sacked-Yards Lost	0-0	2-13
Punts	2-46	5-37
Fumbles-Lost	1-1	2-1
Penalties-Yards	3-15	10-69
Time of Possession	37:57	22:03

RUSHING

Dallas: Richards 16-82, E. Smith 19-67, Martin 1-8, Agee 1-1.
Detroit: Sanders 18-108, Peete 2-9, Kramer 1-6, Stradford 1-1.

PASSING

Dallas: Aikman 16-25-1-214, Beuerlein 2-2-0-26.
Detroit: Peete 6-10-2-69, Kramer 3-7-1-21.

RECEIVING

Dallas: Irvin 5-114, Harper 3-61, Novacek 3-29, E. Smith 3-13, Johnston 3-9, Roberts 1-14.
Detroit: Moore 4-57, Farr 2-14, Campbell 1-10, Perriman 1-6, Sanders 1-3.

MISSED FIELD GOALS

None.

LOUIS DELUCA

PEETE AND RE-PEETE Leon Lett (78, above) and Jim Jeffcoat meet at the quarterback with a sandwich sack of the Lions' Rodney Peete, and Tony Casillas (right) gets in on the fun on another play. The Cowboys hold Peete and the Lions to 201 yards.

LOUIS DELUCA

SOMEONE TO AVOID Despite the lop-sided score, the Lions' Melvin Jenkins puts some painful hits on Cowboys receivers. Above, he sends Michael Irvin sprawling head-first to the artificial turf after a catch. At left, Jenkins runs into Kelvin Martin, who was back to field a punt. The latter play earned Jenkins a penalty for fair-catch interference.

STOPPED OR NOT Just as Cleveland
Gary had predicted days before, the
supposedly lowly Rams are too much
for the Cowboys to handle. Gary
(above) runs through Darren Woodson's arm tackle to score one of his
two touchdowns. At right, cornerback
Robert Bailey (29) runs down Kelvin
Martin after a reception.

NOV. 15, 1992 • TEXAS STADIUM The Los Angeles Rams arrived at Texas Stadium disguised as a powder puff. They left looking like a powerhouse.

In a shocking display of role reversal, the 3-6 Rams upset the 8-1, two-touchdown-favored Cowboys. The Rams scissored two streaks during a 27-23 victory: their 12-game losing binge on the road and the Cowboys' 11-game sequence of home triumphs.

"They met the challenge, and we didn't," defensive tackle Russell Maryland said. "I think it gave them an added boost to come here and play the so-called No. 1 team."

Said linebacker Ken Norton: "We didn't come out with our normal intensity. We didn't have that fire, and I can't figure out why."

The Cowboys also never figured out how to stop Jim Everett or even slow him. Everett, the Rams' inconsistent quarterback, completed 22 of 37 passes for 251 yards and two touchdowns without being intercepted against the NFL's top-ranked defense.

"It's exactly what he used to do against the 49ers," said Charles Haley, who bi-annually faced Everett when playing for San Francisco.

"He always comes in and plays a team he's not supposed to beat and does a great job. This is the NFL. You can be riding high, and somebody will always knock you down."

Everett's success could be traced to leisure time in the pocket. He was not sacked and seldom pressured. Safety James Washington noted the coincidence of a diminished pass rush and Haley's groin pull, rendering him a no-tackle factor.

"It just shows that with a healthy Haley, we're a dominating defense, and without a healthy Haley we're not," Washington said.

The normally precise Cowboys offense had little to show in the way of scoring touch. It manufactured only one touchdown on Emmitt Smith's record-breaking, three-yard dive.

Lin Elliott's foot and Kevin Martin's legs accounted for 16 points on three field goals and a 74-yard punt return. Michael Irvin's huge receiving output (eight catches, 168 yards) went for naught.

So did a messy two-minute drill that died at the Rams' 14-yard line at the final gun. Confusion reigned as Troy Aikman missed two passes. The last pass one-hopped through the end zone. What *was* that final play?

"An incompletion," Aikman snapped.

Smith's touchdown was his 13th rushing to set a club season record. He was not impressed.

"What about it?" he said. "It don't mean nothin'. A lot of things mean more than setting records. Winning is one of them. I'd rather be in the Super Bowl than setting records."

And so he would eventually.

TIME RUNNING OUT Jimmy Johnson wears a worried look as the clock ticks down on his Cowboys. "I don't know that we played poorly, but the Rams played very well," he would say.

DONNA BAGBY

GAME 10

LA RAMS	**27**
DALLAS	**23**

RANDY GALLOWAY

Nov. 16 column:

In the big picture, Dallas lost no NFC East ground as the "toughest division in football" took it on the collective ear Sunday. And the proper response by the Cowboys in coming weeks would mean this is a defeat that set them up mentally for the season's stretch run. But will there be the proper response? That's what makes Sunday's game at Phoenix the biggest of the year.

END OF A ROLL

The last time the Cowboys…

■ lost to a team with a losing record:
Dec. 30, 1990, at Atlanta (26-7).

■ lost at home:
Sept. 15, 1991, to Philadelphia (24-0).

■ allowed a 100-yard rushing game at home:
Oct. 13, 1991, by Cincinnati's Harold Green (124 yards)

■ failed to generate a turnover:
Jan. 5, 1992, at Detroit (playoff defeat)

■ were outgained in yards:
Sept. 20, 1992, by Phoenix (438-413)

■ gave up as many as 27 points:
Oct. 5, 1992, at Philadelphia (31-7)

■ trailed in time of possession:
Oct. 19, 1992, to Kansas City (30:47-29:13)

BLACK SUNDAY FOR NFC EAST

The Cowboys' loss to the Rams cost them no ground in the NFC East race, as all five teams lost:

NFC East team	Rec.	Lost to
Dallas	8-2	LA Rams, 27-23
Philadelphia	6-4	Green Bay, 27-24
Washington	6-4	Kansas City, 35-16
NY Giants	5-5	Denver, 27-13
Phoenix	3-7	Atlanta, 20-17

KEEPING SCORE Both teams make big plays, but the Rams execute more of them. Tony Zendejas (10, above) signals his go-ahead field goal good in the fourth quarter. His kick overcame a 23-21 lead that Kelvin Martin (83, above right) had given the Cowboys with a 74-yard punt return for a touchdown. At right, Aaron Cox gets a step on Issiac Holt (30) down the sideline for a big gain.

ERICH SCHLEGEL

LA RAMS	7	14	0	6 –	27
DALLAS	3	10	10	0 –	23

FIRST QUARTER
LA Rams: Gary 1 run (Zendejas kick), 7:10.
Dallas: FG Elliott 37, 9:44.
SECOND QUARTER
Dallas: Smith 3 run (Elliott kick), :34.
Dallas: FG Elliott 42, 6:59.
LA Rams: Chadwick 8 pass from Everett (Zendejas kick), 12:45.
LA Rams: Gary 3 pass from Everett (Zendejas kick), 14:42.
THIRD QUARTER
Dallas: FG Elliott 36, 5:02.
Dallas: Martin 74 punt return (Elliott kick), 13:49.
FOURTH QUARTER
LA Rams: FG Zendejas 33, 4:31.
LA Rams: FG Zendejas 44, 13:06.
Attendance: 63,690.

TEAM STATS

	LA	Dallas
First downs	24	19
Rushes-yards	32-123	19-80
Passing	244	269
Return Yards	5	81
Comp-Att-Int	22-37-0	22-37-0
Sacked-Yards Lost	1-7	1-3
Punts	4-37	3-43
Fumbles-Lost	0-0	1-0
Penalties-Yards	2-10	7-60
Time of Possession	33:28	26:32

RUSHING

LA Rams: Gary 29-110, Everett 1-6, Turner 1-5, Thompson 1-2.
Dallas: E. Smith 19-80.

PASSING

LA Rams: Everett 22-37-0-251.
Dallas: Aikman 22-37-0-272.

RECEIVING

LA Rams: Gary 7-44, Chadwick 4-38, Anderson 3-77, Cox 2-26, Carter 2-26, Ellard 2-23, Price 1-10, Lang 1-7.
Dallas: Irvin 8-168, Novacek 5-27, Martin 4-51, Johnston 2-13, E. Smith 2-8, Harper 1-5.

MISSED FIELD GOALS

None.

JOHN F. RHODES

FITS AND STARTS Coming off their upset loss to the Rams, the Cowboys find themselves in another dogfight at Phoenix. Alvin Harper (80) is an unlikely hero, scoring the decisive touchdown (above) on a 37-yard reception. It is his first trip to the end zone since the opener against Washington. Troy Aikman (right) passes for 237 yards but is less effective on the ground, as rookie nose tackle Keith Rucker pulls him down after a short gain.

NOV. 22, 1992 • SUN DEVIL STADIUM In an oddball game in which Emmitt Smith caught 11 more passes than Michael Irvin, the Cowboys squeezed past the Phoenix Cardinals, 16-10.

The squeeze went both ways. The Cowboys, coming off their upset home loss to the Los Angeles Rams, had to sweat this one out.

"We were fortunate," coach Jimmy Johnson said.

Fortune smiled early and late on the Cowboys. Three plays in particular went their way. The first was a rib injury to Phoenix quarterback Chris Chandler, forcing rusty and ineffective Timm Rosenbach into three quarters of duty.

"That was a big, big play in more ways than one," Johnson said.

GAME 11

The second crisis arose when Aeneas Williams ran 78 yards with a Troy Aikman pass to give Phoenix an apparent 14-3 lead. But wait. After a long huddle, the officials ruled that Kelvin Martin, the intended target, had touched Williams while he was down. The touchdown was recalled.

In the meantime, Phoenix ganged its defense to stop Smith on the ground and Irvin through the air. Cornerback Robert Massey forewarned Irvin, held to one catch, that he was a special target.

"I asked Massey before the game what they were going to do," Irvin said. "He said, 'Whatever we do, you ain't gonna be a part of it.'"

Others took up the slack. Smith caught 12 short passes, one shy of Lance Rentzel's club record for one game. And Alvin Harper caught the winner, a 37-yard touchdown from Aikman, Harper's first scoring pass since the opener.

"I had to have a big game to keep the coaches on my side so they'd have confidence to throw me the ball," Harper said.

On defense, the Cowboys also had to fill a noticeable hole. Charles Haley remained in Dallas to rehabilitate a leg injury. Holding the Cardinals to 149 yards offense in his absence gave his defensive teammates a deep sense of satisfaction.

"Charles is a talented player," linebacker Ken Norton said, "but we have a lot of talented players on defense. It's about time people start noticing that."

Among them was the pappy-guy of the defensive line, 31-year-old Jim Jeffcoat. Returning to the field where he starred for Arizona State, Jeffcoat frolicked with two sacks, a forced fumble and a team-high seven tackles.

"People kind of got down on us without Charles," he said, "but I think we proved we're a pretty good defense without him."

Defensive coordinator Dave Wannstedt put it this way: "The whole group made a statement that we're not a one-man show."

The Cowboys were partly a rookie show. Lin Elliott kicked his ninth consecutive successful field goal. Cornerback Kevin Smith, the Cowboys' No. 1 draft choice from Texas A&M, made his first NFL start.

The Cowboys were getting younger. And better.

OPPOSITE REACTIONS Tim McDonald (46) isn't quite as happy as Jay Novacek over Novacek's seven-yard touchdown catch seconds before halftime. The play puts the Cowboys in front for good, although their defense has to make the lead stand up in the second half.

JOHN F. RHODES

DALLAS 16
PHOENIX 10

JIMMY JOHNSON
"We were fortunate."

RANDY GALLOWAY
Nov. 23 column:

To all the football civilians out there, go ahead and honk if you still hate the three-man rush. But don't ever complain about never seeing it work. "People confuse it with the prevent – it's *not* a prevent," said Coach Jimmy Johnson, after a 16-10 Dallas victory that was about as pleasant as three hours of root-canal work. The best thing about it for the Cowboys was when it was over.

MICHAEL IRVIN
"We'll laugh, giggle and joke the whole way home. It's always a tough game when we play Phoenix. Let's get the heck out of here."

HOW TIMES CHANGE
Some major differences from the first Cowboys-Cardinals game Sept. 20 to the second Nov. 22:

Category	Sept. 20	Nov. 22
Michael Irvin receiving	8-210 yds	1-18 yds
Randall Hill receiving	5-109	1-18
Chris Chandler passing	24-43-0, 383	35-7-0, 38
Emmitt Smith rushing	26-112	23-84
Alvin Harper receiving	1-14	5-88
Cardinals total offense	438	149

DALLAS	0	10	6	0 – 16
PHOENIX	7	0	0	3 – 10

FIRST QUARTER
Phoenix: Centers 2 pass from Chandler (Davis kick), 8:29.
SECOND QUARTER
Dallas: FG Elliott 28, 7:49.
Dallas: Novacek 7 pass from Aikman (Elliott kick), 14:46.
THIRD QUARTER
Dallas: Harper 37 pass from Aikman (kick failed), 12:32.
FOURTH QUARTER
Phoenix: FG Davis 20, 11:12.
Attendance: 72,439.

TEAM STATS

	Dallas	Phoenix
First downs	18	9
Rushes-yards	30-97	18-46
Passing	237	103
Return Yards	48	100
Comp-Att-Int	25-36-1	15-24-0
Sacked-Yards Lost	0-0	2-15
Punts	5-39	6-44
Fumbles-Lost	0-0	2-1
Penalties-Yards	5-40	5-34
Time of Possession	36:09	23:51

RUSHING

Dallas: E. Smith 23-84, Aikman 4-6, Johnston 2-6, Richards 1-1.
Phoenix: J. Johnson 12-45, Bailey 2-1, Rosenbach 4-0.

PASSING

Dallas: Aikman 25-36-1-237.
Phoenix: Chandler 5-6-0-38, Rosenbach 10-17-0-80.

RECEIVING

Dallas: E. Smith 12-67, Harper 5-88, Novacek 5-50, Irvin 1-18, Johnston 1-8, Martin 1-6.
Phoenix: Centers 5-28, Bailey 3-34, A. Edwards 3-24, J. Johnson 2-12, Hill 1-18, Rolle 1-2.

MISSED FIELD GOALS

None.

JOHN F. RHODES

MANHANDLED With the offense sputtering, the Cowboys' No. 1-ranked defense spends the day defending tenuous leads. Rookie safety Darren Woodson (28) flings Larry Centers to the turf after a short gain, and Jim Jeffcoat's sack forces emergency quarterback Timm Rosenbach to fumble (right, top photo). Emmitt Smith (22, right) tries to outrun Dave Duerson and Jock Jones (55) to the corner.

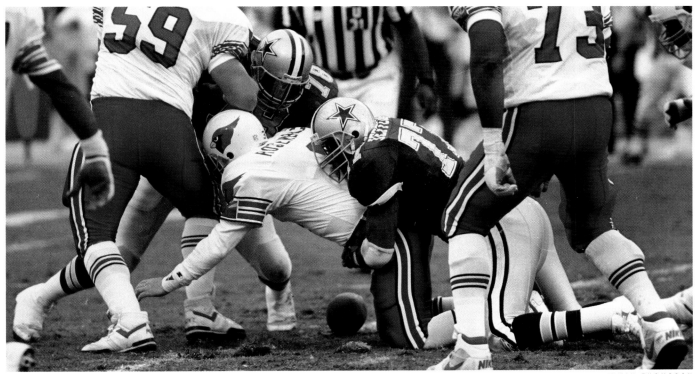

MANY THANKS Tony Tolbert (92) and his defensive teammates aren't the most gracious of hosts to rookie quarterback Kent Graham and the Giants on Thanksgiving Day. Emmitt Smith (right) helps put the turkey in the oven in the third quarter with a 68-yard touchdown run.

NOV. 26, 1992 • TEXAS STADIUM The Cowboys claimed the 300th victory in franchise history – and then halfway apologized for it.

In such ways was long- and short-range progress measured. A player who won one game in 1989 issued style points for a victory.

Guard Nate Newton gave a 30-3 drone over the New York Giants low marks as Thanksgiving Day theater. He put the proper spin on a nationally televised game that will be little noted nor long remembered.

A great deal of messing around took place in the first half as the Cowboys inched ahead, 9-3. This was what Newton had in mind afterward.

"We were kind of sloppy in the first half," he said. "I apologize to America if people were sleeping in the first half instead of eating, like I would have been."

GAME 12

DALLAS   **30**
NY GIANTS   **3**

Two Emmitt Smith gems served as a wakeup call. He turned Troy Aikman's safety-valve pass into a 26-yard touchdown and two minutes later ran 68 yards for another score.

The Giants were impressed.

"I think he's one of the greatest runners of all time," defensive end Leonard Marshall said. "I think he's a good as Walter Payton, maybe better."

Smith rushed for 120 yards and gained another 41 on six pass receptions. He became the first Cowboy to rush for more than 100 yards against the Giants in 12 years. Thanks to smothering blocks ahead of him, his 68-yarder broke so clean the Giants never laid a finger on him.

"I hope they show that to all the high school kids," Newton said. "That was picture perfect. Everybody was on somebody. John Gesek and Erik Williams blew those people away."

Some Giants blew their stacks after the game. They accused the Cowboys of running up the score and of abusive blitzing against rookie quarterbacks Kent Graham and Dave Brown.

"We've never tried to run the score up against Dallas or take any shots against them, even when Aikman was a rookie," Marshall fumed.

The Cowboys were motivated to maintain defensive pressure by memory of their first encounter against New York. Behind 34-0, the Giants stormed back to make a 34-28 game of it behind since-injured Phil Simms.

"We didn't want what happened in the Meadowlands to be repeated," safety James Washington said. "We wanted to show people we could play defense for four quarters."

Graham, the starter, was of unknown quality. Defensive line coach Butch Davis said the Cowboys wanted to pressure him early and often.

"We felt like if we didn't, it might be a long day," he said. "You never know how a rookie is going to react in a situation like this."

Two more rookie quarterbacks lay waiting in Denver. They would not prove as easy prey.

HAND OVER FOOT Larry Brown is the first to congratulate Lin Elliott after his 53-yard field goal gives the Cowboys a 9-0 lead. Elliott's kick is his 12th consecutive successful attempt, setting a club record.

JOHN F. RHODES

RAY HANDLEY
Giants coach when asked if he thought the Cowboys ran up the score:
"No comment."

LEONARD MARSHALL
Giants defensive end:
"I'm leaving with a bitter taste in my mouth. We'll remember this."

BLACKIE SHERROD
Nov. 27 column:
On a day when fancy vittles were the menu, a glass of buttermilk stole the show. Typically, no one noticed. With fancy pies and that evil whipped cream on the Thanksgiving sideboard, who watches cornbread? But that was the Dallas Cowboys' offense against the limping Giants. Downhome cooking.

COWBOYS AT 10-2
Beating the Giants, 30-3, left the Cowboys 10-2, tying the club's best record after 12 games. How they finished the previous four seasons they started 10-2:

Year	Record*	Finish
1968	12-2	Lost Eastern final to Cleveland, 31-20
1976	11-3	Lost division playoff to LA Rams, 14-12
1977	12-2	Won Super Bowl XII over Denver, 27-10
1983	12-2	Lost wild-card playoff to LA Rams, 24-17

* Record at end of regular season.

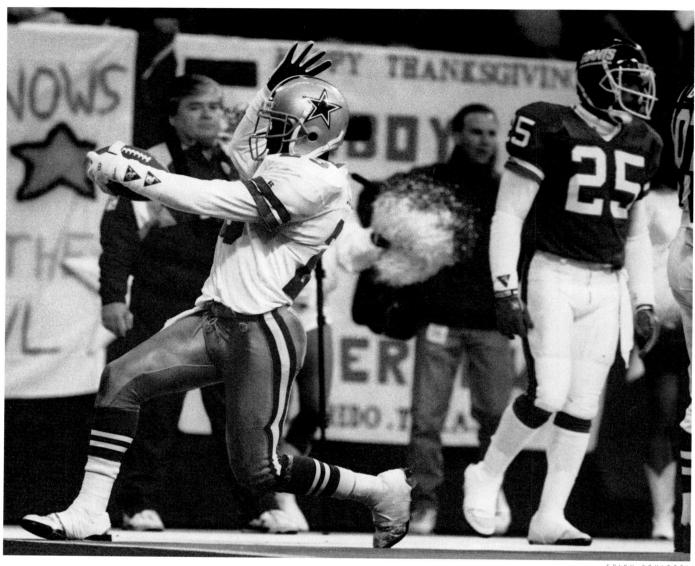

STEPS AND STUMBLES Kenneth Gant (above) shows off "The Shark." Daryl Johnston isn't able to dance away from Giants safety Greg Jackson but still manages to pick up a first down on one of his three receptions for 30 yards.

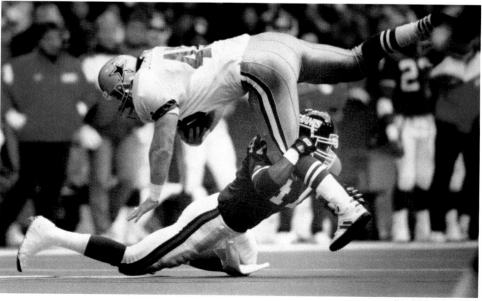

| NY GIANTS | 0 | 3 | 0 | 0 – 3 |
| DALLAS | 3 | 6 | 14 | 7 – 30 |

FIRST QUARTER
Dallas: FG Elliott 45, 11:38.
SECOND QUARTER
Dallas: FG Elliott 33, 2:21.
Dallas: FG Elliott 53, 12:38.
NY Giants: FG Bahr 42, 14:57.
THIRD QUARTER
Dallas: E. Smith 26 pass from Aikman (Elliott kick), 8:57.
Dallas: E. Smith 68 run (Elliott kick), 11:07.
FOURTH QUARTER
Dallas: Harper 4 pass from Aikman (Elliott kick), 8:56.
Attendance: 62,416.

TEAM STATS

	NY	Dallas
First downs	12	17
Rushes-yards	22-80	30-157
Passing	127	142
Return Yards	29	59
Comp-Att-Int	14-31-0	19-29-1
Sacked-Yards Lost	4-30	1-1
Punts	8-37	3-45
Fumbles-Lost	2-1	0-0
Penalties-Yards	11-80	7-68
Time of Possession	25:24	34:36

RUSHING
NY Giants: Hampton 10-33, Meggett 3-22, Bunch 6-20, Graham 2-4, Brown 1-1.
Dallas: E. Smith 17-120, Richards 8-32, Aikman 2-7, Johnston 1-1, Beuerlein 2-(minus 3).

PASSING
NY Giants: Graham 12-28-0-151, Brown 2-3-0-6.
Dallas: Aikman 19-29-1-143.

RECEIVING
NY Giants: McCaffrey 6-105, Calloway 2-15, Hampton 2-13, Meggett 2-13, Cross 2-11.
Dallas: E. Smith 6-41, Irvin 4-37, Johnston 3-30, Novacek 3-22, Harper 2-15, Richards 1-(minus 2).

MISSED FIELD GOALS
NY Giants: Bahr 35, 44.

FEELING LOW Kent Graham picks himself off the turf after recovering a bad snap, dwarfed by teammate Dave Meggett and the Cowboys' Ken Norton and Charles Haley.

TOM FOX

THROWING AND CATCHING Troy Aikman
(above), getting off a pass in front of
Denver's Shane Dronett (99) and Kenny
Walker, completes six of seven throws
on the decisive scoring drive. Alvin
Harper (80, right), normally an Aikman
target, turns defensive back for a play
to intercept Tommy Maddox's Hail
Mary attempt.

DEC. 6, 1992 • MILE HIGH STADIUM This was a game played at Mile High Stadium altitude containing an equally high degree of risk.

Denver coach Dan Reeves took all the risks, but it was the Cowboys who earned the reward of a thrilling 31-27 victory.

Coach Jimmy Johnson's team hiked its record to 11-2 to qualify for the playoffs as no worse than a wild-card entrant. The result left Johnson delighted and defensive coordinator Dave Wannstedt dizzy.

"We expected to be in the play-offs prior to the season and during the season, so that expectation never changed," Johnson said.

Wannstedt didn't know what to expect after Reeves trick-played the Cowboys off their feet behind a rookie quarterback shuttle of Tommy Maddox and Shawn Moore.

"We were kept off balance all day," Wannstedt said. "They were hitting us with so many gadgets, I never had a handle on what they were doing."

Reeves wrung the maximum from a flea-flicker, a halfback option pass, draw plays, screens and shovel passes. "We were fortunate ol' No. 7 wasn't playing today," said Troy Aikman, referring to injured quarterback John Elway.

The Cowboys also were blessed to have Aikman in comeback form. He led a 77-yard drive that Emmitt Smith capped with a three-yard run with 2:47 to play. The winning touchdown was Smith's 16th of the season, tying a club record that Reeves had set in 1966.

Smith scored on a heady, third-down call by offensive coordinator Norv Turner. Turner discarded pass plays to send Smith across on a draw that broke between an anticipated blitz.

"They hadn't blitzed us much," Turner said, "but we saw on film that they liked that down there."

The late rally pleased Aikman, perhaps easing the sting of a late rally gone sour three weeks earlier against the Los Angeles Rams.

"It's more satisfying when it happens this way," he said.

Aikman completed six of seven passes on the final march to make it happen. Teammate Michael Irvin offered a ringing tribute:

"Did you see how he kept his cool? He didn't force it. He kept taking what they would give him. I'll tell you what. There ain't many doing it any better."

Despite their problems, the Cowboys' defense had its best day of the season claiming turnovers. Four of the five were interceptions against Maddox, including a rare pick by receiver-turned-defender Alvin Harper.

"If you take away those trick plays, they lose big," said cornerback Kevin Smith, with typical rookie logic. Take away rain, and there'd be no flood.

And just when they least expected it, rain was about to fall on the Cowboys' parade.

| DALLAS | 31 |
| DENVER | 27 |

GAME 13

RANDY GALLOWAY

Dec. 7 column:

The No. 1 defense in the league? No, not even close. For their own good, the statistical wizards from the league office need to be told the truth. The numbers lie, OK?

IRWIN THOMPSON

FLYING HIGH Emmitt Smith's three-yard touchdown run with 2:47 to play proves doubly satisfying. It provides the Cowboys' margin of victory and is Smith's 16th of the season, tying Dan Reeves' club record. Reeves, ironically, watches from the opposite sideline as the Broncos' coach.

EYES LEFT The Broncos generally hold Emmitt Smith in check, but here he runs through Karl Mecklenburg's tackle for a first down. Smith carries 26 times for only 62 yards.

| DALLAS | 14 | 3 | 7 | 7 – 31 |
| DENVER | 7 | 6 | 7 | 7 – 27 |

FIRST QUARTER
Dallas: Irvin 6 pass from Aikman (Elliott kick), 3:45.
Dallas: Irvin 4 pass from Aikman (Elliott kick), 6:58.
Denver: V. Johnson 18 pass from Maddox (Treadwell kick), 12:29.
SECOND QUARTER
Denver: Jackson 12 pass from Maddox (kick failed), 0:45.
Dallas: FG Elliott 53, 11:35.
THIRD QUARTER
Dallas: Novacek 1 pass from Aikman (Elliott kick), 6:38.
Denver: Rivers 23 pass from Maddox (Treadwell kick), 12:55.
FOURTH QUARTER
Denver: Tillman 81 pass from Marshall (Treadwell kick), 5:55.
Dallas: E. Smith 3 run (Elliott kick), 12:13.
Attendance: 74,946.

TEAM STATS

	Dallas	Denver
First downs	22	15
Rushes-yards	32-82	19-93
Passing	222	261
Return Yards	37	32
Comp-Att-Int	25-35-0	18-31-4
Sacked-Yards Lost	2-9	4-28
Punts	4-46	2-49
Fumbles-Lost	2-0	2-1
Penalties-Yards	7-35	7-67
Time of Possession	37:47	22:13

RUSHING
Dallas: E. Smith 26-62, Aikman 6-20.
Denver: Lewis 10-59, Moore 4-24, Rivers 3-8, Maddox 2-2.

PASSING
Dallas: Aikman 25-35-0-231.
Denver: Maddox 10-17-4-104, Moore 7-13-0-104, Marshall 1-1-0-81.

RECEIVING
Dallas: Novacek 7-87, Irvin 6-62, E. Smith 6-45, Johnston 3-18, Harper 2-17, Martin 1-2.
Denver: V. Johnson 4-71, Rivers 4-38, Jackson 3-39, Sharpe 3-16, Lewis 2-25, Tillman 1-81, Marshall 1-19.

MISSED FIELD GOALS
Dallas: Elliott 32.

IRWIN THOMPSON

NO FURTHER REVIEW A stranger-by-the-second play at Washington's RFK Stadium delays the Cowboys' clinching of the NFC East title. The Redskins' Jason Buck (99, above) starts the mess with a hit that knocks the ball loose from Troy Aikman, who had set up to pass from his end zone. After a mad scramble that includes yet another fumble, Danny Copeland (26, right) finally emerges with clear possession and a Washington touchdown – over the protests of Cowboys coach Jimmy Johnson (opposite page).

DEC. 13, 1992 • RFK STADIUM Upon further review, it's still two fumbles on the same play, a Washington Redskins recovery in the end zone for the winning touchdown and a loopy 20-17 loss for the Cowboys.

Every replay of this raucous wrangle will fasten on a weird play that prevented the Cowboys from clinching the NFC East title. It was a moment worthy of recall. So was the highly suspicious play itself.

However, in the absence of instant replay, field officials allowed the sequence to stand. Troy Aikman was ruled to have fumbled as he tried to pass from the end zone. Had his arm been judged moving forward with football attached, he would have been charged with an incomplete pass.

WASHINGTON 20
DALLAS 17

His arm was moving forward, the officials decided, but without the ball.

Rather than cover Aikman's fumble for a safety, teammate Emmitt Smith tried to scoop it out of the end zone to Alfredo Roberts. The ball bounced free again until the Redskins' Danny Copeland dug it out from the bottom of a pile.

What had been a 17-13 Cowboys lead flipped to 20-17 in Washington's favor with 3:14 to play. And that was it.

"I've seen some weird ones over the years," defensive end Jim Jeffcoat said, "but this is probably at the top of the list."

Linemate Tony Casillas framed the defeat in a few words: "It's a game where we beat ourselves. We did exactly what we needed to do on defense. I felt like we were the better team."

Redskins quarterback Mark Rypien even hinted at agreement.

"We were very fortunate," he said, after passing for only 144 yards. "It's not like we did a lot of good things out there."

Ahead 17-7 at the half and 17-10 after three quarters, the Cowboys donated turnovers on three fourth-quarter possessions. Andre Collins' interception of Aikman, after the Cowboys had driven to the Washington two-yard line with 13 minutes left, began the drift into defeat. Collins' 59-yard return set up a Chip Lohmiller field goal.

"You make three turnovers on three possessions, and you're going to lose. They made us pay for it," said Michael Irvin, a fumble victim.

An excellent game by tight end Jay Novacek lay buried in the debris. He caught two touchdown passes and saved another by catching Collins from behind on the interception runback.

Novacek also prolonged a Cowboys' scoring drive with a heads-down play. Redskins linebacker Wilber Marshall drew a roughing penalty for throwing Novacek on his noggin.

"I was wondering if he was trying out for All-Star Wrestling," Novacek said. "That was a pretty good body slam."

The Cowboys accepted their fate with more determination than distress. Said Aikman: "I think we'll be fine. We've bounced back from losses this year."

And bounce back they would. Higher than any Cowboys team in the past 14 years.

JOHN F. RHODES

RANDY GALLOWAY

Dec. 14 column:

Put this one right up there among the all-time cherished moments for the Cowboys-Redskins rivalry. But the Redskins, of course, will remember it more fondly. Washington by 20-17 was impossible but true. Luckily, nobody passed a torch to (Jimmy) Johnson afterward. He would have used it. ...More importantly, the Cowboys still have breathing room on the schedule to make amends. There were too many positives Sunday for one awful loss to be considered a total negative.

ED WERDER

Dec. 14 turning point story:

"I had a hold of it at one point, and then it was gone," (Troy) Aikman said. He referred to the football, but that would have been an apt description of the lead the Cowboys built and protected for nearly 57 minutes.

REFEREE BOB MCELWEE

On Troy Aikman's end-zone fumble that turned into Washington's decisive touchdown:

"The football got hit by a defender, and I didn't see the arm coming forward with the football clearly in his possession, so I've got to rule fumble."

JOHN F. RHODES

DALLAS	3	14	0	0 –	17
WASHINGTON	0	7	3	10 –	20

FIRST QUARTER
Dallas: FG Elliott 23, 9:57.
SECOND QUARTER
Dallas: Novacek 5 pass from Aikman (Elliott kick), 4:51.
Washington: Orr 41 pass from Byner (Lohmiller kick), 6:47.
Dallas: Novacek 5 pass from Aikman (Elliott kick), 14:51.
THIRD QUARTER
Washington: FG Lohmiller 32, 10:01.
FOURTH QUARTER
Washington: FG Lohmiller 22, 7:58.
Washington: Copeland recovered fumble in end zone (Lohmiller kick), 11:46.

Attendance: 56,437.

TEAM STATS

	Dallas	Wash.
First downs	22	14
Rushes-yards	29-121	25-68
Passing	221	178
Return Yards	26	76
Comp-Att-Int	23-35-1	13-30-1
Sacked-Yards Lost	4-24	2-7
Punts	4-40	5-37
Fumbles-Lost	4-3	0-0
Penalties-Yards	5-37	6-56
Time of Possession	32:14	27:46

RUSHING

Dallas: E. Smith 25-99, Johnston 2-16, Martin 1-5, Aikman 1-1.
Washington: Byner 19-69, Sanders 1-3, Ervins 2-0, Rypien 3-(minus 4).

PASSING

Dallas: Aikman 23-35-1-245.
Washington: Rypien 12-29-1-144, Byner 1-1-0-41.

RECEIVING

Dallas: E. Smith 5-16, Irvin 5-105, Novacek 5-25, Harper 4-51, Martin 3-33, Johnston 1-15.
Washington: Clark 4-50, Sanders 3-53, Orr 2-46, Byner 2-19, Monk 1-9, Ervins 1-8.

MISSED FIELD GOALS

None.

ERICH SCHLEGEL

SACKED AND SADDENED Despite leading almost the entire game, the Cowboys leave Washington with their third loss of the season. Troy Aikman, being sacked by rookie Shane Collins (91, opposite page), is downcast only briefly. Emmitt Smith (22, left), in the clutches of the Redskins' Monte Coleman, runs for 99 yards but is held to fewer than 100 for the fifth time in six games.

TITLE BOUND Emmitt Smith (above) puts his moves on Falcons safety Scott Case (25). Smith would score his club-record 17th touchdown and run for 174 yards, moving within five yards of NFL leader Barry Foster of Pittsburgh. At right, Ken Norton gives the Cowboys an immediate break, stripping the ball from receiver Mike Pritchard on the Falcons' first play from scrimmage.

DEC. 21, 1992 • GEORGIA DOME Everything fell right for the Cowboys on a Monday night in Georgia. Club records, a division title and the Atlanta Falcons descended their way.

Of course, it helped that the Cowboys pushed.

The Georgia Dome became the site of the Cowboys' first NFC East title clinching in seven years, their 14th title overall and a bye week in the playoffs ahead. A 41-17 rout of the Falcons made it emphatic fact.

All of the Cowboys' big offensive guns fired. Troy Aikman completed 18 of 21 passes for 239 yards and three touchdowns. He strung together a career-best 13 consecutive completions.

"Aikman did a fantastic job. He put it right on the money," Coach Jimmy Johnson said.

Emmitt Smith rushed for 174 yards and scored a club-record 17th touchdown. As an underline, Smith did it on a 29-yard run on which he engaged a nest of four tacklers, bounced off, then scooted home.

Smith also gained ground in another direction. He pulled within five yards of Pittsburgh's Barry Foster for the NFL rushing lead.

"I can't say enough about their running back. He's a heck of a player," Atlanta coach Jerry Glanville praised. "The Cowboys did a really good job in everything. They just whipped us."

Jay Novacek set a club season record for tight ends with his 69th reception. On and on went the Cowboys. Atlanta linebacker Jessie Tuggle watched the traffic in disbelief.

"Dallas is a great team," he said. "They have so many weapons – Aikman, Smith, all through the lineup. I give them a lot of credit. I hit Smith hard, but it just backed him up three or four steps, and he was able to get away."

Three plays to begin the second half catapulted the Cowboys from a 20-10 lead into 34-10 command. Aikman threw a 23-yard touchdown pass to Alvin Harper. Thomas Everett covered a kick-return fumble by Deion Sanders. Smith followed with his dazzler into the end zone.

"I don't know if that was the turning point," Johnson said. "I don't know if there was a turning point, other than we had the better football team. The whole team really clicked."

Yet there was work to be done. A regular-season finale against Chicago offered a shot at a franchise-best 13 victories in a season. Would Smith beat Foster to repeat as the NFL rushing leader? Could the Cowboys maintain their momentum?

"We're proud of this team," Johnson said. "This is an accomplishment, but we've got a lot of football left."

Spoken like a coach who foresaw even more success falling into place during his first championship season.

DALLAS 41
ATLANTA 17

WINNING TRADITION

The Cowboys are one of four NFL teams to have won 10 or more division championships since the 1970 NFL-AFL merger:

Team	Titles
San Francisco	11
Dallas	10
Minnesota	10
Pittsburgh	10

RANDY GALLOWAY

Dec. 22 column:

And then (Atlanta coach Jerry) Glanville had the bright idea of sticking Deion Sanders on Michael Irvin. ...A few more one-on-one games against Irvin, and the Atlanta Braves will find themselves with a full-time outfielder.

TROY AIKMAN

On completing 18 of 21 passes for 239 yards and three touchdowns:

"Atlanta has the kind of defense that puts pressure on you, and they have two outstanding corners. I certainly didn't come into the game anticipating the kind of success I had. It worked well for me."

SHIRTING THE ISSUE

By the end, mostly Cowboys fans remain at the Georgia Dome, celebrating their team's division title triumph with an Emmitt Smith replica jersey.

JUAN GARCIA

DALLAS	3	17	14	7 —	41
ATLANTA	7	3	0	7 —	17

FIRST QUARTER
Dallas: FG Elliott 47, 5:29.
Atlanta: Hill 6 pass from Wilson (Johnson kick), 9:39.
SECOND QUARTER
Dallas: Martin 11 pass from Aikman (Elliott kick), 0:53.
Dallas: FG Elliott 22, 8:46.
Dallas: Novacek 18 pass from Aikman (Elliott kick), 13:46.
Atlanta: FG Johnson 27, 15:00.
THIRD QUARTER
Dallas: Harper 23 pass from Aikman (Elliott kick), 3:10.
Dallas: E. Smith 29 run (Elliott kick), 3:35.
FOURTH QUARTER
Dallas: E. Smith 29 run (Elliott kick), 2:45.
Atlanta: Rison 10 pass from Wilson (Johnson kick), 6:45.

Attendance: 67,036.

TEAM STATS

	Dallas	Atlanta
First downs	19	18
Rushes-yards	29-196	11-40
Passing	239	335
Return Yards	11	13
Comp-Att-Int	18-21-0	34-46-0
Sacked-Yards Lost	0-0	4-37
Punts	2-53	2-50
Fumbles-Lost	0-0	4-3
Penalties-Yards	7-50	3-24
Time of Possession	33:05	26:55

RUSHING

Dallas: E. Smith 24-174, Harper 1-15, Richards 3-5, Agee 1-2.
Atlanta: Broussard 4-17, Wilson 2-15, T. Smith 2-9, K. Jones 2-3, Sanders 1-(minus 4).

PASSING

Dallas: Aikman 18-21-0-239.
Atlanta: Wilson 30-41-0-342, Tolliver 4-5-0-30.

RECEIVING

Dallas: Irvin 6-89, Novacek 5-69, Harper 3-53, Martin 2-23, E. Smith 2-5.
Atlanta: Pritchard 9-105, Hill 9-84, Rison 6-45, Haynes 5-100, K. Jones 2-21, Broussard 2-12, Milling 1-5.

MISSED FIELD GOALS

Dallas: Elliott 46.

STANDING TALL Solid pass protection helps Troy Aikman complete 18 of 21 for 239 yards. He throws for three touchdowns with no interceptions, beginning a stretch of efficiency that will carry through the playoffs.

BIG FINISH Emmitt Smith emerges from the stadium tunnel after his 31-yard touchdown run in the third quarter that also clinched his second consecutive NFL rushing title. "I knew what I needed," he said. "It was nice to get it all in one shot – the touchdown, the rushing title." How the NFL's top three rushers fared on the final Sunday:

Emmitt Smith, Dallas

15-game total	1,582
16th game	131
Season yards	1,713

Barry Foster, Pittsburgh

15-game total	1,587
16th game	103
Season yards	1,690

Thurman Thomas, Buffalo

15-game total	1,390
16th game	98
Season yards	1,488

ERICH SCHLEGEL

DEC. 27, 1992 • TEXAS STADIUM A game of marginal consequence became an event of significant undertow and aftershock as the Cowboys and Chicago Bears closed the regular season.

The Bears lost despite having two head coaches on the premises. One was Mike Ditka, on his way out after 11 seasons that included a Super Bowl championship in 1985.

Defiant before the end, Ditka said: "I'm not sure where the line is to apologize, but I won't be in it."

The other Chicago head coach happened to be in the Cowboys' coaching booth upstairs. Defensive coordinator Dave Wannstedt was on his way in, although no one knew at the time that he would be named Ditka's successor a few weeks later.

Emmitt Smith was on his way back to the top. Knowing he needed 109 yards to overtake Barry Foster of Pittsburgh for a repeat NFL rushing title, Smith gained 131 to finish with 1,713.

Mike Singletary was on his way out the door after 12 superb seasons as the Bears' middle linebacker. The former All-America from Baylor and future NFL Hall of Famer retired at the final gun.

Therein lay the emotional tug of the Cowboys' 27-14 victory. A franchise-record 13th victory added milestone pleasure to the occasion.

The aftershock centered around Smith's backup, Curvin Richards. He fumbled twice in the fourth quarter to help whittle a 27-0 lead. One was returned 42 yards by Chris Zorich for a Chicago touchdown.

"I was not happy with the sloppy play," Coach Jimmy Johnson snapped. "I am never happy with sloppy play, I don't care what the score is."

A man of his testy word, Johnson released Richards the next day.

The Cowboys also scored a defensive touchdown of extravagant note. Tackle Russell Maryland ran 26 yards after a mid-air recovery of Darren Lewis' fumble.

Maryland, a Chicago native, celebrated in the end zone with a backward spike, followed by a belly-flop and a tinge of chagrin at the show.

"I didn't know what to do," he said. "Kenny Gant has the 'Shark' move. I guess that was the 'Killer Whale.' And that was the first and last time you'll see it."

Closing regular season 13-3 and as NFC East champions, the Cowboys faced a bye week before a playoff opener at home. Their opponent was unknown, to be drawn from a qualifying cast of Minnesota, New Orleans and Philadelphia.

"The 13 wins means a lot to us," Troy Aikman said, "but the most important thing was winning the East. In the playoffs, our record won't mean a thing.

"Throw everything else out the window. Our season's success will be measured on what we do in the playoffs."

DALLAS 27
CHICAGO 14

GAME 16

RUSSELL MARYLAND

"We were real disappointed we lost the shutout late. But the important thing is that we won and we have the No. 1 defense (in the NFL)."

TIM COWLISHAW

Dec. 28 sidebar story:

There are two reasons Curvin Richards is No. 2 on the Cowboys' depth chart (at halfback). One is Emmitt Smith. The other is Curvin Richards.

BEARING WITNESS A toy teddy bear, attached by the neck to a Cowboys' flag, is a lonely spectator to the Cowboys' 13th victory.

ERICH SCHLEGEL

| CHICAGO | 0 | 0 | 0 | 14 – 14 |
| DALLAS | 0 | 3 | 24 | 0 – 27 |

SECOND QUARTER
Dallas: FG Elliott 21, 13:56.
THIRD QUARTER
Dallas: E. Smith 31 run (Elliott kick), 3:55.
Dallas: Maryland 26 fumble return (Elliott kick), 4:26.
Dallas: Richards 3 run (Elliott kick), 8:49.
Dallas: FG Elliott 34, 13:48.
FOURTH QUARTER
Chicago: Green 6 run (Butler kick), 2:30.
Chicago: Zorich 42 fumble return (Butler kick), 5:41.
Attendance: 63,101.

TEAM STATS

	Chicago	Dallas
First downs	9	22
Rushes-yards	15-28	44-179
Passing	64	175
Return Yards	32	80
Comp-Att-Int	9-23-3	18-31-1
Sacked-Yards Lost	2-25	1-2
Punts	7-44	2-44
Fumbles-Lost	2-1	4-3
Penalties-Yards	6-50	1-15
Time of Possession	18:01	41:59

RUSHING
Chicago: Anderson 3-17, Green 3-11, Muster 2-5, Lewis 7-(minus 5).
Dallas: E. Smith 20-131, Agee 9-30, Richards 13-22, Beuerlein 2-(minus 4).

PASSING
Chicago: Furrer 9-23-3-89.
Dallas: Aikman 10-20-0-78, Beuerlein 8-11-1-99.

RECEIVING
Chicago: Morgan 5-53, Jennings 2-17, Davis 1-13, Lewis 1-6.
Dallas: Irvin 5-46, Novacek 3-39, Johnston 3-24, Harper 2-38, E. Smith 2-8, Martin 1-10, Agee 1-6, Richards 1-6.

MISSED FIELD GOALS
Dallas: Elliott 28.

FITFUL START Charles Haley and his defensive cohorts make Will Furrer's first NFL start less than memorable. Furrer (2), a rookie from Virginia Tech, is buried under Haley's rush (left) and then barely can get out of the way as Haley swats down a pass (above). The Bears manage only 92 yards, and Furrer is intercepted three times.

ERICH SCHLEGEL

JAN. 10, 1993 • TEXAS STADIUM If not a perfect game, the Cowboys' playoff performance against the Philadelphia Eagles ranked as a reasonable facsimile. By whatever measure, it was too good for the Eagles.

This was a game the Cowboys had waited two weeks to play and were in a hurry to win. They made haste to win in no-contest style, 34-10, and earn an NFC Championship Game berth against the San Francisco 49ers at Candlestick Park.

"This was a complete, total win for our organization, from Jerry Jones all the way down," Coach Jimmy Johnson said. "We were just ready to play, and that was very evident."

A Cowboys' playoff victory at Texas Stadium had been a long time coming. The last one belonged to the 1982 team that beat Green Bay, 37-26.

The Eagles scored first on a field goal and last on a pass with 50 seconds left. The Cowboys scored 34 points in between with a near-flawless display that impressed even the distressed Eagles.

"How do I explain what happened? That's pretty easy," said guard Brian Baldinger, a former Cowboy. "Dallas beat our butts. We got beat by a superior team, without any questions asked. I don't think there's a man on this team who won't tell you the same thing."

Eagles quarterback Randall Cunningham was among those who agreed after the Cowboys sacked him five times and held him to 160 yards passing.

"They deserve all the credit, and I don't think they get all the credit they do deserve," he said.

Center David Alexander added final emphasis: "They are obviously a great team and will be a great team for a while. We thought they would be about the same team we played last time, but that was not the case. They are a lot better."

The more the Cowboys played the Eagles, the better they got. This was the third in a series that began the fourth week of the teams' regular season with a 31-7 Philadelphia rout. The Cowboys won the return at home, 20-10, and followed with a rubber-match crusher.

Cowboys safety Thomas Everett noted the trend. Present-day shock may lead to future psych when the Eagles and Cowboys reconvene in fall 1993.

"We did a number on them today, and they will be thinking about it until we play 'em again," he said.

The highest number belonged to an offense that riddled the Eagles for 346 yards. Emmitt Smith rushed for 114, making him the first to surpass 100 against Philadelphia's proud defense in 56 games. He also gained the last word against Eagles safety Andre Waters, who spent a good part of the preceding week trading barbs and threats.

Troy Aikman (15-of-25, two touchdowns) blended flawless passing. Aikman's confidence, in himself and his team, soared to new heights.

"We have confidence we can play with anybody," he said. "That's not to say we're going to beat everybody we play. It doesn't work that way. But if we play well on both sides of the ball, we like our chances against anyone in the league."

One of Aikman's scoring passes was a one-yard lob to tight end Derek Tennell, who signed five days earlier to replace injured blocking specialist Alfredo Roberts. So fooled were the Eagles that the closest figure to the newcomer was a Cowboy Cheerleader.

"I was a little surprised they called my number," Tennell said. "I was thinking, 'Don't drop the darn thing. You can be the biggest hero or the biggest goat when you're that open. Just catch it.'"

Tennell caught his first pass as a Cowboy. The Cowboys caught the Eagles. Their next quest lay to the west in soggy San Francisco.

TAKE THE HIGH ROAD Emmitt Smith, his valuable legs very much intact, uses them to soar over the Eagles' Byron Evans (56) and John Booty on a first-quarter run. Smith would run for 114 yards, becoming the first back to surpass 100 against the Philadelphia defense in 56 games.

DALLAS   34
PHILADELPHIA   10

DIVISIONAL PLAYOFF

BLACKIE SHERROD
Jan. 11 column:
Normally, at a large playoff game as this one between the Iggles and Your Heroes, you count the grizzles and grayhairs on each side and weigh them with great care. Experience is the surest teacher. The formula didn't work this time out. The kids won the picnic from here to the parking lot and back. I think the fire marshal estimated the loss at 34-10, but he may have been on the conservative side.

RANDY GALLOWAY
Jan. 11 column:
Bearhugs, victory whoops and wide-lens grins dominated the post-game locker room festivities at Texas Stadium. For this team, that's about the equivalent of New Year's Eve in Rio.

EMMITT SMITH
On Eagles safety Andre Waters:
"He had an awful lot to say once he got into the game. ...One time I carried the ball and heard him saying, 'Hold him up, hold him up, I want to get a shot at him.' He was saying, 'I'm going to break your leg.' ...That kept up the whole game, except right at the end. I didn't hear much from him at the end of the game."

ANDRE WATERS
On Emmitt Smith:
"No, I didn't talk to him. I came here to play football. This is a business trip, not a time to chit-chat."

RIGHT AT HOME Not every millionaire-businessman can walk the sidelines at Texas Stadium and play cheerleader, but Jerry Jones (top photo), after all, owns the joint. After the pre-game balloons (left), Frank Lauria (above, left) and Calvin Jones of Plano respond. Troy Aikman (opposite page) gives them more to cheer with two touchdown passes.

FLAT-OUT ROUT Tony Tolbert is too much for Randall Cunningham to handle (pages 92-93) on one of the Cowboys' five sacks. Hounded and pounded, Cunningham throws for only 160 yards.

PHILADELPHIA	3	0	0	7 –	10
DALLAS	7	10	10	7 –	34

FIRST QUARTER
Philadelphia: FG Ruzek 32, 7:15.
Dallas: Tennell 1 pass from Aikman (Elliott kick), 13:02.
SECOND QUARTER
Dallas: Novacek 6 pass from Aikman (Elliott kick), 14:13.
Dallas: FG Elliott 20, 15:00.
THIRD QUARTER
Dallas: E. Smith 23 run (Elliott kick), 3:44.
Dallas: FG Elliott 43, 11:43.
FOURTH QUARTER
Dallas: Gainer 1 run (Elliott kick), 11:41.
Philadelphia: C. Williams 18 pass from Cunningham (Ruzek kick), 14:10.
Attendance: 63,721.

TEAM STATS

	Phil.	Dallas
First downs	12	22
Rushes-yards	17-63	38-160
Passing	115	186
Return Yards	24	5
Comp-Att-Int	17-30-0	15-25-0
Sacked-Yards Lost	5-45	2-14
Punts	7-41	4-43
Fumbles-Lost	4-2	2-1
Penalties-Yards	6-76	5-30
Time of Possession	24:43	35:17

RUSHING
Philadelphia: Walker 6-29, Cunningham 5-22, Sherman 6-12.
Dallas: E. Smith 25-114, Gainer 9-29, Aikman 3-13, Johnston 1-4.

PASSING
Philadelphia: Cunningham 17-30-0-160.
Dallas: Aikman 15-25-0-200.

RECEIVING
Philadelphia: Walker 6-37, C. Williams 4-48, Barnett 4-44, Byars 3-31.
Dallas: Irvin 6-88, Novacek 3-36, Martin 3-27, Harper 1-41, Johnston 1-7, Tennell 1-1.

MISSED FIELD GOALS
None.

JOHN F. RHODES

JOHN F. RHODES

HIGH AND TIGHT Alvin Harper (above) gives it his best but can't quite reach this Troy Aikman pass. The Cowboys get the yards, however, as cornerback Eric Allen, running stride for stride with Harper, is flagged for interference. At left, Derek Tennell (89) rushes to congratulate Jay Novacek on his six-yard touchdown catch that gives the Cowboys a 14-3 lead.

ESCORT SERVICE Kelvin Martin's shifty moves on a 39-yard return (above) leave the Eagles' kick-coverage unit chasing, sprawling and banging into each other. At left, Jimmy Johnson has plenty of company as he walks away with his second NFL playoff triumph.

JIMMY JOHNSON

"I felt like we would win before the game started. ...It's a big win for us. We've got bigger wins coming."

RANDALL CUNNINGHAM

Eagles quarterback

"They are a great team. And today, they whipped our butts. They're a young team, and they'll be around for a while, so we and others had better get used to them."

JAN. 17, 1993 • CANDLESTICK PARK Elements no one could control and a long-ago playoff dominated the prelude to the NFC Championship Game between the Cowboys and San Francisco 49ers.

Undue worry about rain and distant recall of a similar Cowboys-49ers contest were preliminary distractions to the main event. Pre-game focus fell upon such disparate characters as George Toma and Dwight Clark.

Toma, the "Sod God" or "Nitty-Gritty Dirt Man," answered an emergency call from the NFL to repair and replace a Candlestick Park turf soaked by weeks of rain. His expert touch would determine whether the game would be played on firm footing or the equivalent of a soap dish.

Clark was the 49er who caught the winning touchdown pass from Joe Montana to beat the Cowboys in the 1981 NFC Championship Game. A rematch 12 years later at the same site revived those memories.

Here's what happened:

Toma repaired The Field.

Clark relived The Catch.

The Cowboys won The Game.

"How 'bout them Cowboys?" was Coach Jimmy Johnson's post-game analysis.

A solid 30-20 victory sent the Cowboys into Super Bowl XXVII against the Buffalo Bills at the Rose Bowl in Pasadena, Calif. It would be the Cowboys' NFL-record sixth Super Bowl appearance and their first since the 1979 club lost to Pittsburgh, 35-31.

"It was a fantastic effort," Johnson said. "Not just today, not just this week, but starting four years ago when we were at rock bottom."

The climb had been steady, swift and amazing. From 1-15 to 7-9 to 12-6 to 15-3 and counting, the Cowboys were back. The earth moved twice, figuratively and literally, as if to offer proof.

The Thursday night before kickoff, the ground shook in Irving as nearly 70,000 fans

DALLAS 30
SAN FRANCISCO 20

NFC CHAMPIONSHIP

BLACKIE SHERROD
Jan. 18 column:
The Cowboys were the team with assurance, with patient precision and poise. The old, unflappable pros. One doesn't suppose, taking it man for man, that the Cowboys are judged superior talent over their hosts. But they certainly performed as if.

RANDY GALLOWAY
Jan. 18 column:
In the beginning, it was Jimmy and Troy, with some very bad football and very bad vibrations. On Sunday, it was happiness and togetherness. In two weeks, it will be the Super Bowl, with Jimmy and Troy and a whole lot more.

TIM COWLISHAW
Jan. 18 game story:
The Cowboys provided no "Catch" per se, but they made catches all day that caught San Francisco unprepared. In the end, the Cowboys did not erase history, but they certainly avoided repeating it…

JAMES WASHINGTON
On the oft-discussed Candlestick Park field:
"It was fine in the middle, but on the sides outside the hash marks, it was sand. It was like playing on the beach. But we're football players. We grew up playing in the streets, running between cars. This was no problem."

LOUIS DELUCA

A DAY TO CELEBRATE To the victors go the hugs. The 49ers' David Whitmore (left) is a solemn spectator as Kelvin Martin receives congratulations for a six-yard touchdown catch. Michael Irvin (above) and John Gesek greet Emmitt Smith after his scoring run in the second quarter.

PEP FOR THE 'BOYS In the grandest of send-offs, an estimated 70,000 fans pack Texas Stadium to salute the Cowboys before they leave for San Francisco. Some stir the air with flags (above), while others, like Jeff Tharp (right) of Grapevine, are just clowning around.

packed Texas Stadium to give their team a Texas-sized, pep-rally send-off.

"This is what football and the NFL is all about," club owner Jerry Jones told the assembled multitudes. Jones, in fact, estimated another 10,000 fans milled outside the stadium, unable to find a seat.

The throng impressed two of the most famous ex-Cowboys from the previous era.

"If we'd had a pep rally like this, we would have beaten the Steelers in Super Bowl XIII," said Roger Staubach, once a quarterback of some note.

"Roger's right. If we'd had this kind of send-off, I don't think we would have ever lost that game," said Tony Dorsett, the previous incarnation of Emmitt Smith. "I don't think there's anything like this in the NFL, and I don't think there ever will be."

Receiver Michael Irvin, representing the current era, was among the Cowboys taking the microphone that night.

"We have more people here than most teams have at football games," he told the cheering, flag-waving fans. "That's why most teams are home and we're going to San Francisco. For those of you I don't see in San Francisco, I'll see you in Pasadena."

The next night, an earthquake rocked the Bay Area, measuring 5.1 on the Richter scale. That would prove to be a mere tremble compared to the eventual Cowboys triumph.

Johnson allowed a brief peek into the past. A team that once dressed in pauper's rags now wore a conference crown.

"Our coaches kept demanding more and more of the players," he said. "When they responded in a positive way, we kept demanding even more. Sometimes the demands may have been unrealistic, yet the players always responded.

"But we have one more game to go."

Irvin was among a small group of players who had taken every comeback step with Johnson and reflected on then and now.

"Not only were we 1-15 four years ago, but people were saying that my career was over after I went through major knee surgery," he said. "It was like I was at the bottom, truly at the bottom, and now I'm one step away from being at the top."

The Cowboys gained their Super Bowl berth with a display of collective excellence against a team rated a one-touchdown betting favorite. Their offense controlled the ball for 35:20 turnover-free minutes. Their defense, No. 1-ranked with nary a Pro Bowl performer, produced two interceptions of league Most Valuable Player Steve Young and two fumble recoveries.

Toma's field received solid reviews. Little rain fell during the game, and the new Bermuda sod down the middle held up fine.

The Cowboys also left their version of The Catch as a counter-memory. The 49ers threatened, rallying to within 24-20 with 4:22 to play after Johnson's fourth-and-inches gamble failed at the San Francisco seven-yard line.

With the momentum again shifting and the 64,920 fans at Candlestick Park back in focus, offensive coordinator Norv Turner made a bold first-down call from the Cowboys' 21.

Instead of trying to run out the clock, Turner dialed a quick slant pass to Alvin Harper, who had made an acrobatic 38-yard reception to set up the Cowboys' go-ahead touchdown early in the third quarter.

With the fourth quarter now ticking away, Harper caught Troy Aikman's bullet and raced 70 yards to set up Kelvin Martin's six-yard clinching touchdown with 3:43 to kill.

Feet churning, Harper raced toward the end zone with his mind fixed on the prize.

"I was saying, 'Man, this is it, we're in the Super Bowl now … it's all over,'" he said. And so they were. How 'bout them Cowboys?

DALLAS	3	7	7	13	– 30
SAN FRANCISCO	7	3	3	7	– 20

FIRST QUARTER
Dallas: FG Elliott 20, 8:20.
San Francisco: Young 1 run (Cofer kick), 11:11.
SECOND QUARTER
Dallas: E. Smith 5 run (Elliott kick), 9:55.
San Francisco: FG Cofer 28, 13:41.
THIRD QUARTER
Dallas: Johnston 4 run (Elliott kick), 4:15.
San Francisco: FG Cofer 42, 8:35.
FOURTH QUARTER
Dallas: E. Smith 16 pass from Aikman (Elliott kick), 2:35.
San Francisco: Rice 5 pass from Young (Cofer kick), 10:38.
Dallas: K. Martin 6 pass from Aikman (kick failed), 11:17.
Attendance: 64,920.

TEAM STATS

	Dallas	SF
First downs	24	24
Rushes-yards	30-121	21-114
Passing	295	301
Return Yards	43	30
Comp-Att-Int	24-34-0	25-35-2
Sacked-Yards Lost	4-27	3-12
Punts	4-36	1-57
Fumbles-Lost	1-0	2-2
Penalties-Yards	4-25	4-38
Time of Possession	35:20	24:40

RUSHING

Dallas: E. Smith 24-114, Johnston 2-7, Harper 1-3, Aikman 3-(minus 3).
San Francisco: Watters 11-69, Young 8-33, Rathman 1-6, Lee 1-6.

PASSING

Dallas: Aikman 24-34-0-322.
San Francisco: Young 25-35-2-313.

RECEIVING

Dallas: E. Smith 7-59, Irvin 6-86, Johnston 4-26, Harper 3-117, Novacek 3-28, K. Martin 1-6.
San Francisco: Rice 8-123, Watters 6-69, Rathman 4-33, Jones 3-40, Taylor 3-33, Sherrard 1-15.

MISSED FIELD GOALS

Dallas: Elliott 43.
San Francisco: Cofer 47.

WING AND A PRAYER On the pivotal play of the third quarter – and perhaps the game – Alvin Harper beats 49ers cornerback Eric Davis for a 38-yard reception to set up the touchdown that gives the Cowboys a 17-10 lead. "I don't know how he did it," Davis said. "It was just great concentration on his part."

SCOTT OSTLER

San Francisco Chronicle, Jan. 18 column
for *The News:*
Left to their own devices, handicapped by
a level playing field and a lack of help
from above, the 49ers lost to a better
team.

CHARLES HALEY

On winning against his former team:
"It's not a personal battle. It's a team
thing. We played well, and that's the key.
The offense put points on the board, and
the defense put pressure on the 49ers."

ALFREDO ROBERTS

"Kevin Smith shut Jerry Rice up."

JOHN F. RHODES

KEN GEIGER

AIKMAN ROLLS A 300
Troy Aikman (above) escapes to pass for 322 yards, his first 300-yard effort of the season and fourth of his career, all on the road:

Date	Opponent	Cmp.-Att.	Yards
Nov. 12, 1989	at Phoenix	21-for-40	379
Nov. 18, 1990	at LA Rams	17-for-32	303
Oct. 27, 1991	at Detroit	28-for-42	331
Jan. 17, 1993	at San Fran.	24-for-34	322

POWER-BACKERS
Ken Norton (51) and Robert Jones sense victory after Norton's fourth-quarter interception.

KEN GEIGER

BACK TO BACK Daryl Johnston (above) and Emmitt Smith (left) help the Cowboys wear down the 49ers in the second half.

OFF WITH HIS HEAD Russell Maryland (pages 104-105, photo by John F. Rhodes) catches the 49ers' elusive Steve Young and wrestles him down after a short scramble. Young, the NFL's Most Valuable Player, is held to 33 yards rushing.

STEPPING LIVELY Ken Norton (above) wades through the thousands of happy fans who jam Dallas/Fort Worth International Airport to welcome the Cowboys back from San Francisco. At left, Jerry Jones captures the sideline spirit after James Washington's interception ensures victory, but Kenny Gant (right) gives the fans the dance they want with his "Shark."

JAN. 31, 1993 • ROSE BOWL Long before the Cowboys arrived in Southern California for Super Bowl XXVII, Coach Jimmy Johnson fixed their minds on how to play it.

"This has been our theme," he said. "We want to play our best game of the year in the last game. And we all know where that last game is."

Mentally armed with a last-game mentality, the Cowboys kept winning until they had no more games to play. They saved their excessive best for a spectacular finale to win Super Bowl XXVII over the Buffalo Bills.

It couldn't have been better than 52-17.

In a rout of astounding scope, the Cowboys scored enough surplus points to win Super Bowl XXVIII. Which, by the way, they are favored to capture. (If you want to get started on travel arrangements, it's Jan. 30, 1994, at the Georgia Dome in Atlanta.)

A Rose Bowl crowd of 98,374 and a record 133.4 million television viewers saw a half-time show starring Michael Jackson and a game dominated full time by the Cowboys. Both had become legends in their own time: Jackson as the world's premier entertainer; the Cowboys as a riches-from-rags team that lost 15 of 16 games only four years ago.

"One of the reasons this is one of the happiest days of my life is that Jimmy and I went through that 1-15 season," Owner Jerry Jones said. "We had some pretty low times together during that year, but I knew one day we'd be the Super Bowl champions."

Winning Super Bowl XXVII was a short time coming from those lean days. It will be a long time worth remembering as the franchise's first Super Bowl triumph since 15 Roman numerals ago, when the 1977 Cowboys beat Denver, 27-10.

In presenting the Lombardi Trophy to Johnson and Jones, NFL commissioner Paul Tagliague said: "You two are the architects, the engineers who produced outstanding seasons capped by an awesome display of football and marking one of the most extraordinary turnarounds in history."

Said Johnson: "There was never any doubt we'd get to this point. The concern was how long it would take."

To the victors went various spoils. Among them were payoffs of $36,000 to each player,

DALLAS 52
BUFFALO 17

SUPER BOWL XXVII

BLACKIE SHERROD

Feb. 1 column:

And in the topper here in the rocking old Rose Bowl, when Superbowl pressure has turned more than one challenger into Jell-O, the Cowboys reached a new high in composure. They were expected to beat the Bills, but not bury them. This 52-17 thing was no trivial disrespect for elders. This was Lizzie Borden, saying hi-dee-ho to her parents, then hacking away with her axe.

RANDY GALLOWAY

Feb. 1 column:

But then they kicked off and played the game. And then it came down to special people, players and coaching staff, responding in this special situation. As they had done two weeks ago at Candlestick (your *real* Super Bowl, Commissioner Tagliabue) and the week before against the Eagles and all those weeks since September, the Cowboys proved they could handle any pressurized scene. Particularly this Super Bowl scene.

GIVING IT AWAY

The Cowboys, in a record six Super Bowl appearances, have the top three performances for turnover takeaways:

Year	Team	Opponent	TD
1993	Dallas	Buffalo	9
1978	Dallas	Denver	8
1971	Dallas	Baltimore	7
1986	Chicago	New England	6

KEN GEIGER

CLOSE UNTIL IT STARTS Fans massing toward the Rose Bowl (above) have no idea of how lopsided a game they are about to witness. Alvin Harper (left) puts an exclamation point on his touchdown by dunking the ball over the crossbar.

STARRY-EYED Super Bowl Sunday in Pasadena, Calif., is the right time and place to be a Cowboys' fan, as some whoop it up (above) and others focus in on the building rout.

awards, future endorsements and a call from the White House. President Clinton phoned Johnson and fellow Arkansas native Jones to offer congratulations.

"He told me he thought the people of Arkansas were prouder of me than they were of him when he became president," Jones said. "I thanked him for the compliment but told him he was just being kind."

Johnson completed a one-of-a-kind hat trick. He became the only coach to win a national college title (Miami, 1987) and Super Bowl and to have played on a national championship team (Arkansas, 1964).

"This has got to be better than winning the national championship and going undefeated because it's a higher level," Johnson said. "The feelings are similar, but this is a notch better."

In true best-for-last fashion, quarterback Troy Aikman won the Super Bowl Most Valuable Player award. He passed with impeccable accuracy (22-of-30, 273 yards, four touchdowns) to finish at an absolute peak.

Aikman became the fifth Cowboy to win or share the MVP trophy. Others were Chuck Howley (V), Roger Staubach (VI) and co-recipients Harvey Martin and Randy White (XII).

Aikman's immense talent meshed during the playoffs. Against the NFL's elite – Philadelphia, San Francisco and Buffalo – he completed 61 of 89 passes (68.5 percent) for 795 yards and eight touchdowns without an interception.

Now the all-time highest-ranked passer in post-season games with a 116.8 rating, Aikman accepted his status with typical moderation.

"I really have not had that game yet where it just went completely beyond anything I imagined," he said. "I didn't realize I had the kind of numbers I did in the Super Bowl, except for the four touchdown passes. Things just kind of evolved."

Things dissolved once again for the AFC champion. This was the ninth consecutive Super Bowl victory for an NFC team and third in succession for an NFC East entrant. In setting a Super Bowl record for appearances, the Cowboys squared their mark at 3-3.

Misapplied psychology led some experts – NBC Sports announcers and *Sports Illustrated,* in particular – to pick Buffalo to upset the 6½-point-favored Cowboys. Those experts reasoned experience in two previous Super Bowls would benefit the Bills.

The perceived strength of their logic contained its weakness. The only Super Bowl experience Buffalo had was how to lose one. Whether by memory or rote, the Bills lost their third consecutive Super Bowl during a record nine-turnover mangle.

"It would have been unrealistic to expect them to put the ball on the ground nine times," center Mark Stepnoski said. "If you take that into consideration, it's amazing the margin of victory wasn't larger."

The final margin could have been 59-10. Officials failed to detect that quarterback Frank Reich had passed the line of scrimmage as he threw a 40-yard touchdown pass to Don Beebe. And Leon Lett, styling too soon at the end of a 64-yard fumble rumble, lost a touchdown when Beebe punched the ball loose and through the end zone for a touchback.

Nevertheless, it was a field day for the no-name field mice of the Cowboys' defense. They scored twice on short fumble returns by linebacker Ken Norton and tackle Jimmie Jones.

"The No-Name defense ... I mean, we don't care," tackle Tony Casillas snorted. "All I can say is we'll have the rock (ring) on our hands."

The best of the rest were two interceptions by Thomas Everett and one apiece by Larry Brown and James Washington off Jim Kelly, who left early with a knee injury, and Reich. Jones covered yet another fumble, as did Clayton Holmes. It was a Jimmy Durante-type show ... everybody wanted to get in on the act.

The Bills wished to get back in a game they trailed, 28-10, at halftime. Reich, after all, had rallied them from a 35-3 deficit to 41-38 overtime victory in a playoff against Houston, and Johnson offered a gruff reminder during locker-room remarks.

"He talked about it, but he didn't talk about it long," guard Nate Newton said. "He said, 'Damn Houston. We ain't Houston. We're the Cowboys.'"

While Buffalo stars Kelly, Bruce Smith, Cornelius Bennett and Thurman Thomas faded, the Cowboys' offensive galaxy produced contrasting glitter.

CINDY YAMANAKA

WALL OF FAME Plenty of fans are there to encourage Ken Norton as he heads toward the field, and Norton and the Cowboys give them plenty to cheer about over the next few hours.

RUSSELL MARYLAND

On losing defensive coordinator Dave Wannstedt (right, with Jimmy Johnson) after the Super Bowl:

"He's a lot more than a coach to us. That was the best way to send him off. We think an awful lot of the guy."

THE JONES GANG Lindy, Layne and Lance Jones do their hair-brained version of Kenneth Gant's "Shark."

Emmitt Smith, the first NFL rushing champ to appear in a Super Bowl, gained 108 yards. Michael Irvin caught six passes for 114 yards and two touchdowns. Alvin Harper and Jay Novacek also grabbed scoring passes. The offensive line worked with precision.

The Bills were dazed.

"We didn't shut them down in the first half, but we slowed them down," linebacker Shane Conlan said. "I don't know what happened after that. It all went blank."

Back home, the streets – virtually deserted while more than eight out of 10 television sets in use tuned into the game – quickly flooded with the faithful. Fans jammed the West End district, forcing police to halt automobile traffic into the area. They danced along Hampton Road in Oak Cliff, where parking lots turned into party spots. Some fans celebrated by firing guns into the air "everywhere, all over the city," a Dallas police dispatcher said.

By 9:30 p.m. Dallas time, the downtown party had spread beyond the West End. Motorists packed city streets, hanging out windows, dancing in pickup truck beds and setting off their car alarms. Honking car horns were audible long into the wee hours.

The Cowboys, of course, were elated start to finish. Particularly at the finish.

"People asked me if I wanted to make a great catch in the last minute," Irvin said. "I said, 'No, I want to see Steve Beuerlein handing the ball to Derrick Gainer and I'm on the sideline dancing.'

"That's the way it happened. Perfect."

The Cowboys paid a price for perfection in advance. The defense lost its coordinator, Dave Wannstedt, already named head coach of the Chicago Bears. Offensive line coach Tony Wise departed with his best friend along with assistant Bob Slowik.

They leave behind not only an NFL champion but the league's youngest team at an average age of 26.6 years. Is a dynasty in place? Buffalo receiver James Lofton thinks so. Asked what might slow the Cowboys in the future, Lofton said:

"An earthquake in Santa Monica tonight … that's the only thing that will stop the Cowboys."

Cowboys elder Jim Jeffcoat agreed. He said the best was yet to come.

"We're on top of the world, and we're not coming off," he said. "You'd better be ready for us, 'cause we're going to be here for a long time."

So began an off-season for the Cowboys in which Johnson will slightly alter the best-for-last theme that served him so well. Far in advance of the 1993 opener, he will remind the Cowboys to begin saving their best for first.

"In my wildest dreams, I never thought about winning a Super Bowl," safety James Washington said. "Where do you go from here? You try to repeat."

JIMMY JOHNSON

"I felt like we had the best football team. When you turn the ball over as many times as they did, you'll have trouble. Sometimes it snowballs."

TROY AIKMAN

"This game means everything to me. A tremendous weight has been lifted from my shoulders. No matter what happens to me the rest of my career, I can say I took a team to the Super Bowl and won it. There aren't too many who can say that. This is as great a feeling as I've ever had in my life."

KEN NORTON

On Buffalo's record nine turnovers:

"Everyone is always talking about our speed, but we are physical. They just weren't dropping the ball, we were knocking it out, taking it away from them. I think we just wanted it a little more than they did."

JERRY JONES

"It feels great to be the best in the world."

NATE NEWTON

After helping Jim Jeffcoat dump the contents of a water cooler over Jimmy Johnson's carefully coifed head:

"What was he going to do to me? Cut me? Not today. We won the Super Bowl."

MICHAEL IRVIN

"Tomorrow we'll start thinking about a repeat. But today, just today, we'll enjoy this. Then I'm sure Jimmy will start this all over again."

PARTY ON, GARTH The XXVIIth Super Bowl lives up to its reputation as more than a game, as celebrities swarm the Rose Bowl. Country-western star Garth Brooks sings the national anthem, with television's Marlee Matlin providing simultaneous sign interpretation (near right). Michael Jackson (far right) hitches up his pants for the half-time spectacular, and the Dallas Cowboys Cheerleaders lend their tight-knit choreography to pre-game festivities.

BUFFALO

DALLAS

RUSHING

Player	No	Yds	Avg	Lng	TD	Player	No	Yds	Avg	Lng	TD
Kenneth Davis	15	86	5.7	14	0	Emmitt Smith	22	108	4.9	38	1
Thurman Thomas	11	19	1.7	9	1	Troy Aikman	3	28	9.3	19	0
Carwell Gardner	1	3	3.0	3	0	Derrick Gainer	2	1	0.5	1	0
Frank Reich	2	0	0.0	0	0	Steve Beuerlein	1	0	0.0	0	0
						Daryl Johnston	1	0	0.0	0	0
Totals	29	108	3.7	14	1	Totals	29	137	4.7	38	1

PASSING

Player	Att	Cmp	Yds	Sks	TD	Lng	Int	Player	Att	Cmp	Yds	Sks	TD	Lng	Int
Jim Kelly	7	4	82	2	0	40	2	Troy Aikman	30	22	273	1	4	45	0
Frank Reich	31	18	194	2	1	40	2								
Totals	38	22	276	4	1	40	4	Totals	30	22	273	1	4	45	0

RECEIVING

Player	No	Yds	Lng	TD	Player	No	Yds	Lng	TD
Andre Reed	8	152	40	0	Jay Novacek	7	72	23	1
Thurman Thomas	4	10	7	0	Michael Irvin	6	114	25	2
Kenneth Davis	3	16	13	0	Emmitt Smith	6	27	18	0
Don Beebe	2	50	40	1	Daryl Johnston	2	15	8	0
Steve Tasker	2	30	16	0	Alvin Harper	1	45	45	1
Pete Metzelaars	2	12	7	0					
Keith McKeller	1	6	6	0					
Totals	22	276	40	1	Totals	22	273	45	4

INTERCEPTIONS

					Player	No	Yds	Lng	TD
None					Thomas Everett	2	12	22	0
					J. Washington	1	13	13	0
					Larry Brown	1	0	0	0
					Totals	4	35	22	0

PUNTING

Player	No	Yds	Avg	Blk	In20	Lng	Player	No	Yds	Avg	Blk	In20	Lng
Chris Mohr	3	136	45.3	0	1	48	Mike Saxon	3	131	43.7	1	2	57
Totals	3	136	45.3	0	1	48	Totals	3	131	32.8	1	2	57

PUNT RETURNS

Player	No	FC	Yds	Lng	TD	Player	No	FC	Yds	Lng	TD
Clifford Hicks	1	1	0	0	0	Kelvin Martin	3	0	35	30	0
Totals	1	1	0	0	0	Totals	3	0	35	30	0

KICKOFF RETURNS

Player	No	Yds	Lng	TD	Player	No	Yds	Lng	TD
Brad Lamb	2	49	33	0	Kelvin Martin	4	79	22	0
Kenneth Davis	1	21	21	0					
Clifford Hicks	1	20	20	0					
Totals	4	90	33	0	Totals	4	79	22	0

FIELD GOALS

Player	M-A	Blk	Dist. missed	Player	M-A	Blk	Dist. missed
Steve Christie	1-1	0	None	Lin Elliott	1-1	0	None
Totals	1-1	0	None	Totals	1-1	0	None

DEFENSIVE STATISTICS

Player	T	A	S	Player	T	A	S	Player	T	A	S	Player	T	A	S
Bennett	8	1	0	Talley	6	0	0	Norton	8	1	0	Haley	5	0	1
Patton	6	0	0	B. Smith	4	1	1	Washington	4	2	0	Edwards	4	2	0
Odomes	4	0	0	Conlan	3	5	0	Maryland	4	2	0	Woodson	4	0	0
Jones	3	2	0	Williams	3	2	0	Lett	3	0	1	Everett	3	0	1
Darby	3	0	0	Wright	3	0	0	Holmes	3	0	0	Casillas	2	3	0
Pike	3	0	0	Kelso	2	2	0	Jeffcoat	2	0	1	Brown	2	0	0
Hanson	2	1	0	Hale	2	0	0	V. Smith	2	0	0	R. Jones	2	0	0
Maddox	1	0	0	K. Davis	1	0	0	Gant	2	1	0	Horton	1	0	0
Beebe	1	0	0	Metzelaars	1	0	0	K. Smith	1	0	0	Holt	1	0	0
Tasker	0	1	0	Goganious	0	1	0	Tolbert	1	0	0	Gainer	1	0	0
								Pruitt	1	0	0				

PASSES DEFENSED
Buffalo: James Williams, Marvcus Patton, Darryl Talley, Bruce Smith, Cornelius Bennett
Dallas: Larry Brown 3, Thomas Everett 2, James Washington, Ken Norton

FUMBLES FORCED
Buffalo: Bruce Smith
Dallas: Leon Lett 2, Charles Haley, Kenneth Gant, Jim Jeffcoat

FUMBLES RECOVERED
Buffalo: Phil Hansen, Rob Awalt, Kenneth Davis, Clifford Hicks
Dallas: Jimmie Jones 2, Leon Lett, Ken Norton, Clayton Holmes, Troy Aikman

T – solo tackles; A – assisted tackles; S – sacks

BUFFALO	7	3	7	0 — 17
DALLAS	14	14	3	21 — 52

FIRST QUARTER
Buffalo: Thomas 2 run (Christie kick), 5:00.
Dallas: Novacek 23 pass from Aikman (Elliott kick), 13:24.
Dallas: Jones 2 fumble return (Elliott kick), 13:39.

SECOND QUARTER
Buffalo: FG Christie 21, 12:36.
Dallas: Irvin 19 pass from Aikman (Elliott kick), 13:06.
Dallas: Irvin 18 pass from Aikman (Elliott kick), 13:24.

THIRD QUARTER
Dallas: FG Elliott 20, 6:39.
Buffalo: Beebe 40 pass from Reich (Christie kick), 15:00.

FOURTH QUARTER
Dallas: Harper 45 pass from Aikman (Elliott kick), 4:56.
Dallas: E. Smith 8 run (Elliott kick), 6:48.
Dallas: Norton 9 fumble return (Elliott kick), 8:29.

Attendance: 98,374

	Buffalo	Dallas
Total First Downs	22	20
Rushing	7	9
Passing	11	11
Penalty	4	0
3rd Down Made-Att.	5-11	5-11
3rd Down Efficiency	.454	.454
4th Down Made-Att.	0-2	0-2
Total Net Yards	362	408
Total offensive plays	71	60
Avg. gain per play	5.1	6.8
Net Yards Rushing	108	137
Total rushing plays	29	29
Avg. gain per rush	3.7	4.7
Net Yards Passing	254	271
Sacks-yards lost	4-22	1-2
Gross yards passing	276	273
Att.-Comp.-Had Int.	38-22-4	30-22-0
Avg. gain per pass	6.0	8.7
Punts-Avg.	3-45.3	4-32.8
Had blocked	0	1
Total Return Yards	0	70
Punt returns-yards	1-0	3-35
Int. returns-yards	0-0	4-35
Kickoff returns-yards	4-90	4-79
Penalties-Yards	4-30	8-53
Fumbles-Lost	8-5	4-2
Touchdowns	2	7
Rushing	1	1
Passing	1	4
Return	0	2
Extra Point Made-Att.	2-2	7-7
Field Goals Made-Att.	1-1	1-1
Time of Possession	28:48	31:12

RUN-AROUND, TOO

Troy Aikman's passing earns him the Most Valuable Player award, but he shows Buffalo's Bruce Smith that he also brings his running shoes (28 yards, three carries). Aikman, however, is only a sidelight to the Cowboys' running game. The star of that show is Emmitt Smith, who drags Mark Kelso for the last chunk of his 12 yards (pages 118-119). Smith's 108 yards make him the 10th back to exceed 100 in a Super Bowl.

CLOSE QUARTERS Jim Kelly's Super
Sunday is short and sour. Charles
Haley (near right) pounds the Buffalo
quarterback on this fluttering attempt. Jay Novacek (far right) is a
sleeve away from breaking a big
play, as Shane Conlan drags him
down. Despite the final score, the
Cowboys' day starts in reverse, with
Steve Tasker's block of a Mike
Saxon punt (lower right) setting up
the game's first score.

KEN GEIGER

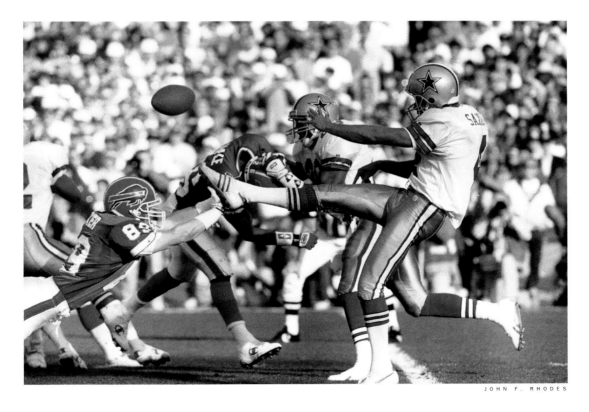

LOUIS DELUCA

CAPITAL D After scoring first, the Bills' offense crumbles in the face of the Cowboys' defensive pressure. Jim Kelly, before leaving in the second quarter with a knee injury, is largely ineffective, as Charles Haley forces a fumble (left) and Russell Maryland runs him down for another sack (lower left). By the third quarter, it's all over but the shouting for Kenneth Gant (29) and his defensive teammates.

LOUIS DELUCA

LOUIS DELUCA

124

CAPITAL O Troy Aikman, behind near-flawless protection from Mark Stepnoski and the offensive line (far left), picks apart the Buffalo defense for 273 yards and four touchdowns. Jay Novacek, trying to wrench free from James Williams (above), scores one, and Michael Irvin (left) put his gloves on two others.

CLEARING THE DECKS James Washington (37, pages 126-127) and the Cowboys' defense use considerable muscle to throw the Buffalo passing game into disarray. James Lofton (80) can't get his hands on this pass and finishes the day with no receptions.

LOUIS DELUCA

HITS, MAN Ken Norton, son of a former heavyweight boxing champion, delivers two of the most pivotal blows of Super Bowl XXVII. After hurdling a blocker, he crashes into Jim Kelly on a sack (above left). The force of Norton's tackle sprains Kelly's right knee, ending his day in the second quarter (left). On the fifth play of the second quarter, with the Cowboys' lead at 14-7, Norton fills the gap on third-and-goal from the one, halting Kenneth Davis (23) in his tracks. The Cowboys intercepted on the next play, and the rout was on.

LOUIS DELUCA

MOST VALUABLE POST-SEASON If quarterbacks are judged by their championships, Troy Aikman (left) makes a compelling case for himself with his almost-flawless post-season run. "Troy had a great game and a great three weeks," offensive coordinator Norv Turner said after the Super Bowl. "You've got to look at his play and let it speak for itself." So here are the numbers:

Opponent	Cmp.	Att.	Yards	Int.	TD
Philadelphia	15	25	200	0	2
at San Francisco	24	34	313	0	2
Buffalo	22	30	273	0	4
Totals	**61**	**89**	**795**	**0**	**8**

A LITTLE PLUCK Thomas Everett, the former Baylor standout acquired from Pittsburgh in September, soars over Buffalo's Pete Metzelaars (88) to make one of his two Super Bowl interceptions. The Cowboys intercepted two other passes and recovered five fumbles to set a Super Bowl record for takeaways with nine.

JOHN F. RHODES

TUGS AND STRUTS Nate Newton, normally a blocker, turns defender to drag down the Bills' James Williams, who nearly has an interception. Jimmie Jones (left) shows off his moves after his fumble recovery and two-yard touchdown return gives the Cowboys a 14-7 lead.

HUNDREDS OF REASONS Buffalo running back Thurman Thomas has another dismal Super Bowl, but at least he keeps his sense of humor. Talking to the Cowboys' Emmitt Smith (above) after the game, Thomas says, "Payday is coming down the line. Go get your money." Smith laughs, but maybe because he already has thought of it. His post-season rushing statistics make a strong case for a big raise:

Opponent	Att.	Yards	Avg.	TD
Philadelphia	25	114	4.6	1
at San Francisco	24	114	4.8	1
Buffalo	22	108	4.9	1
Totals	**71**	**336**	**4.7**	**3**

RUNDOWN FEELING Thurman Thomas
may be the NFL's best all-purpose back,
but doesn't show it against the Cowboys. He scores the opening touchdown
by squirting between blockers on a two-
yard run (above), but the rest of his day
goes downhill fast. He finishes with 19
yards on 11 carries.

TOUCHING DOWN Michael Irvin (pages
136-137, photo by Erich Schlegel) dives
to finish off his 18-second, two-touch-
down flurry that puts the Bills in a 28-10
hole at halftime. On this score, Irvin
again victimizes Nate Odomes (37).

ALL-STAR SPECTACULAR A trio of the Cowboys' Pro Bowl performers give the Bills fits. Jay Novacek (above) turns upfield on one of his team-leading seven receptions. With the Cowboys' line negating standout rusher Bruce Smith (78, right), Troy Aikman has time to pick and choose his targets. And Michael Irvin (far right) is joyous after scoring one of his two second-quarter touchdowns.

CINDY YAMANAKA

ERICH SCHLEGEL

SOARING AND SOLEMN Alvin Harper (far left) prepares to pull in Troy Aikman's 45-yard touchdown pass that puts the Cowboys in front, 38-17, early in the fourth quarter, as at the other end of the field, Aikman (above) begins his celebration. After the game, the Bills' Mark Kelso (38) and Pete Metzelaars pray.

ACTION, REACTION Emmitt Smith (far left) charges through the Bills' defense on his eight-yard touchdown run in the fourth quarter that makes it 45-17. As the final seconds tick away, Michael Irvin becomes the hugmaster, wrapping up Jimmy Johnson (above) and Smith (middle left). Across the field, Thurman Thomas reflects a decidedly different mood. And amid post-game fireworks (pages 144-145, photo by Cindy Yamanaka), Irvin and Alvin Harper are the picture of joy.

JOHN F. RHODES

LOUIS DELUCA   KEN GEIGER

ERICH SCHLEGEL

THE TROPHY CLUB Emmitt Smith (left) puts a bearhug on the Vince Lombardi Trophy, symbolic of pro football's world championship. Jerry Jones and Jimmy Johnson (above) take their turn with the coveted prize in the raucous post-game locker room.

DAVID WOO

TOM FOX

ERICH SCHLEGEL

FACES IN THE CROWD Jerry Jones (above) acknowledges the cheers of the thousands of Cowboys fans who descended on downtown Dallas for the Super Bowl victory parade Feb. 9. Super Bowl MVP Troy Aikman (far left), surrounded by police and minicams, tips his cap to the fans. A Dallas officer drives through a blizzard of confetti while trying to control the enthusiastic crowd lining Commerce Street.

ERICH SCHLEGEL

DAVID WOO

DAY TO REMEMBER The huge crowd, estimated at more than 300,000, eventually caused control problems for Dallas police. Fans surge into Commerce Street, slowing the procession of convertibles carrying Cowboys players and coaches (far left), and some celebrants wanted to be the first to feel the falling confetti (near left). Above, fans descend on City Hall Plaza for the post-parade ceremony. Sporadic violence broke out after the ceremony, as roving bands of youths caused physical and property damage in the downtown area.

COWBOYS REGULAR-SEASON STATISTICS

APPENDIX Ia

TEAM

	Dallas	Opponents
Total First Downs	324	241
Rushing	119	68
Passing	183	147
Penalty	22	26
3rd Down Made-Att.	87-208	50-184
3rd Down Efficiency	41.8	27.2
4th Down Made-Att.	8-12	7-15
Total Net Yards	5,606	3,933
Total offensive plays	1,014	873
Avg. gain per play	5.5	4.5
Net Yards Rushing	2,121	1,244
Total rushing plays	500	345
Avg. gain per rush	4.2	3.6
Net Yards Passing	3,485	2,689
Sacks-yards lost	23-112	33-347
Gross yards passing	3,597	3,036
Attempts-Comp.	491-314	484-263
Had Intercepted	15	17
Avg. gain per pass	7.3	6.3
Punts-Average	61-43.0	87-42.1
Had blocked	0	2
Return Yards	708	697
Punt returns-yards	44-550	34-397
Int. returns-yards	17-158	15-300
Kickoff returns-yards	37-699	60-1,217
Penalties-Yards	91-650	94-727
Fumbles-No. Lost	16-9	25-14
Touchdowns	48	29
Rushing	20	11
Passing	23	16
Return	5	2
Extra Point Made-Att.	47-48	27-29
Field Goals Made-Att.	24-35	14-17
Avg. Time of Possession	33:57	26:03

INDIVIDUAL

PASSING

Player	Att.	Com.	Com. Pct.	Yards	Avg. Gain	TD	TD Pct.	Int.	Int. Pct.	Lng	Rtng
Troy Aikman	473	302	63.8	3,445	7.28	23	4.9	14	3.0	87t	89.5
Steve Beuerlein	18	12	66.7	152	8.44	0	0.0	1	5.6	27	69.7
TEAM	491	314	64.0	3,597	7.33	23	4.7	15	3.1	87t	88.8
OPPONENTS	484	263	54.3	3,036	6.27	16	3.3	17	.5	81t	69.9

RUSHING

Player	Att.	Yards	Avg.	Lng	TD
Emmitt Smith	373	1,713	4.6	68t	18
Troy Aikman	37	105	2.8	19	1
Daryl Johnston	17	61	3.6	14	0
Tommie Agee	16	54	3.4	10	0
Alvin Harper	1	15	15.0	15	0
Kelvin Martin	2	13	6.5	8	0
Steve Beuerlein	4	-7	-1.7	-1	0
Michael Irvin	1	-9	-9.0	-9	0
Other	49	176	3.6	15	1
TEAM	500	2,121	4.2	68t	20
OPPONENTS	345	1,244	3.6	28	11

RECEIVING

Player	No	Yards	Avg.	Lng	TD
Michael Irvin	78	1,396	17.9	87t	7
Jay Novacek	68	630	9.3	34	6
Emmitt Smith	59	335	5.7	26t	1
Alvin Harper	35	562	16.1	52	4
Kelvin Martin	32	359	11.2	27	3
Daryl Johnston	32	249	7.8	18	2
Alfredo Roberts	3	36	12.0	18	0
Tommie Agee	3	18	6.0	8	0
John Gesek	1	4	4.0	4	0
Other	3	8	2.7	6	0
TEAM	314	3,597	11.5	87t	23
OPPONENTS	263	3,036	11.5	81t	16

INTERCEPTIONS

Player	No	Yards	Avg.	Lng	TD
James Washington	3	31	10.3	16	0
Kenneth Gant	3	19	6.3	11	0
Thomas Everett	2	28	14.0	17	0
Ray Horton	2	15	7.5	15t	1
Issiac Holt	2	11	5.5	8	0
Kevin Smith	2	10	5.0	7	0
Larry Brown	1	30	30.0	30	0
Godfrey Myles	1	13	13.0	13	0
Alvin Harper	1	1	1.0	1	0
TEAM	17	158	9.3	30	1
OPPONENTS	15	300	20.0	59	0

PUNTING

Player	No	Gross Yds	Avg	Net Avg	In 20	Lng
Mike Saxon	61	2,620	43.0	33.5	19	58
OPPONENTS	87	3,660	42.1	35.1	17	73

PUNT RETURNS

Player	No	FC	Yards	Avg.	Lng	TD
Kelvin Martin	42	18	532	12.7	79t	2
Ray Horton	1	0	1	1.0	1	0
Kevin Smith	1	0	17	17.0	17	0
TEAM	44	18	550	12.5	79t	2
OPPONENTS	34	6	397	11.7	65	0

KICKOFF RETURNS

Player	No	Yards	Avg.	Lng	TD
Kevin Martin	24	503	21.0	59	0
Clayton Holmes	3	70	23.3	28	0
Kevin Smith	1	9	9.0	9	0
Dixon Edwards	1	0	0.0	0	0
Others	8	117	14.6	21	0
TEAM	37	699	18.9	59	0
OPPONENTS	60	1,217	20.3	42	0

SCORING BY QUARTERS

	1	2	3	4	OT	Total
Dallas	108	116	134	51	0	409
OPPONENTS	54	53	51	85	0	243

FIELD GOALS

Player	1-19	20-29	30-39	40-49	50+
Lin Elliott	0-0	6-7	10-14	5-10	3-4
OPPONENTS	1-1	4-4	4-5	5-7	0-0

SCORING

Player	TD Run	TD Rec	TD Ret	XP M-A	FG M-A	Saf	Pts
Lin Elliott	0	0	0	47-48	24-35	0	119
Emmitt Smith	18	1	0	0-0	0-0	0	114
Michael Irvin	0	7	0	0-0	0-0	0	42
Jay Novacek	0	6	0	0-0	0-0	0	36
Kelvin Martin	0	3	2	0-0	0-0	0	30
Alvin Harper	0	4	0	0-0	0-0	0	24
Daryl Johnston	0	2	0	0-0	0-0	0	12
Troy Aikman	1	0	0	0-0	0-0	0	6
Ray Horton	0	0	1	0-0	0-0	0	6
Russell Maryland	0	0	1	0-0	0-0	0	6
Robert Williams	0	0	1	0-0	0-0	0	6
Issiac Holt	0	0	0	0-0	0-0	1	2
Other	1	0	0	0-0	0-0	0	6
TEAM	20	23	5	47-48	24-35	1	409
OPPONENTS	11	16	2	27-29	14-17	0	243

DEFENSIVE

Player	T	A	S	Player	T	A	S
Norton	64	56	0	K. Smith	22	9	0
R. Jones	55	53	1	Holt	23	7	0
Washington	51	44	0	Lett	13	13	3.5
Tolbert	46	41	8.5	J. Jones	14	9	4
V. Smith	33	36	1	Myles	12	9	0
Brown	45	16	0	Bates	5	6	0
Everett	27	31	0	Edwards	5	5	0
Casillas	28	27	3	R. Williams	5	2	0
Gant	33	21	3	Pruitt	3	2	0
Maryland	26	23	2.5	Hennings	1	1	0
Jeffcoat	23	19	10.5	Holmes	1	0	0
Haley	21	18	6	Hill	0	1	0
Horton	18	16	0	Others	4	1	0
Woodson	28	5	1				

T – solo tackles; A – assisted tackles; S – sacks

INDIVIDUAL

PASSING

Player	Att	Com	Yds	TD	Int	Lng
Troy Aikman	89	61	795	8	0	70
TEAM	**89**	**61**	**795**	**8**	**0**	**70**
OPPONENTS	**103**	**64**	**749**	**3**	**6**	**40t**

RUSHING

Player	No	Yds	Avg.	Lng	TD
Emmitt Smith	71	336	4.7	38	3
Troy Aikman	9	38	4.2	19	0
Daryl Johnston	4	11	2.8	4	1
Alvin Harper	1	3	3.0	3	0
Steve Beuerlein	1	0	0.0	0	0
Derrick Gainer	11	30	2.7	9	1
TEAM	**97**	**418**	**4.3**	**38**	**5**
OPPONENTS	**67**	**285**	**4.3**	**16**	**1**

RECEIVING

Player	No	Yds	Avg.	Lng	TD
Michael Irvin	18	288	16.0	33	2
Jay Novacek	13	136	10.5	23	2
Emmitt Smith	13	86	6.6	18	1
Alvin Harper	5	203	40.6	70	1
Kelvin Martin	4	33	8.3	12	1
Daryl Johnston	7	48	6.9	10	0
Derek Tennell	1	1	1.0	1t	1
TEAM	**61**	**795**	**13.0**	**70**	**8**
OPPONENTS	**64**	**749**	**11.7**	**40**	**3**

INTERCEPTIONS

Player	No	Yds	Avg.	Lng	TD
James Washington	2	34	17.0	21	0
Thomas Everett	2	12	6.0	22	0
Ken Norton	1	14	14.0	14	0
Larry Brown	1	0	0.0	0	0
TEAM	**6**	**70**	**11.7**	**22**	**0**
OPPONENTS	**0**	**0**	**0.0**	**0**	**0**

PUNTING

Player	No	Gross Yds	Avg	Net Avg	In 20	Lng
Mike Saxon	11	445	40.5	33.7	2	57
OPPONENTS	**11**	**479**	**43.5**	**35.5**	**5**	**57**

PUNT RETURNS

Player	No	FC	Yds	Avg.	Lng	TD
Kelvin Martin	5	1	48	9.6	30	0
James Washington	1	0	0	0.0	0	0
TEAM	**6**	**1**	**48**	**8.0**	**30**	**0**
OPPONENTS	**8**	**2**	**54**	**6.8**	**15**	**0**

KICKOFF RETURNS

Player	No	Yds	Avg.	Lng	TD
Kelvin Martin	9	201	22.3	39	0
Kevin Smith	1	11	11.0	11	0
TEAM	**10**	**212**	**21.2**	**39**	**0**
OPPONENTS	**15**	**314**	**20.9**	**50**	**0**

SCORING BY QUARTERS

	1	2	3	4	OT	Total
Dallas	24	31	20	41	0	116
OPPONENTS	**17**	**6**	**10**	**14**	**0**	**47**

FIELD GOALS

Player	1-19	20-29	30-39	40-49	50+
Lin Elliott	0-0	3-3	0-0	1-2	0-0
OPPONENTS	**0-0**	**2-2**	**1-1**	**1-2**	**0-0**

SCORING

Player	TD Run	TD Rec	TD Ret	XP M-A	FG M-A	Saf	Pts
Lin Elliott	0	0	0	14-15	4-5	0	26
Emmitt Smith	3	1	0	0-0	0-0	0	24
Michael Irvin	0	2	0	0-0	0-0	0	12
Jay Novacek	0	2	0	0-0	0-0	0	12
Kelvin Martin	0	1	0	0-0	0-0	0	6
Alvin Harper	0	1	0	0-0	0-0	0	6
Daryl Johnston	1	0	0	0-0	0-0	0	6
Derrick Gainer	1	0	0	0-0	0-0	0	6
Derek Tennell	0	1	0	0-0	0-0	0	6
Jimmie Jones	0	0	1	0-0	0-0	0	6
Ken Norton	0	0	1	0-0	0-0	0	6
TEAM	**5**	**8**	**2**	**14-15**	**4-5**	**0**	**116**
OPPONENTS	**2**	**3**	**0**	**5-5**	**4-5**	**0**	**47**

DEFENSIVE

Player	T	A	S	Player	T	A	S
Norton	15	6	0	Lett	5	5	1
Brown	15	3	0	Jeffcoat	7	1	2
Everett	9	6	1	Edwards	5	2	0
Casillas	7	7	3	Tolbert	4	3	2
K. Smith	11	2	0	Gant	4	2	0
R. Jones	8	5	0	Holmes	3	0	0
V. Smith	5	8	0	J. Jones	1	2	0
Maryland	8	4	2	Pruitt	2	0	0
Washington	8	4	0	Holt	1	1	0
Woodson	10	1	0	Horton	1	0	0
Haley	8	2	1				

T – solo tackles; A – assisted tackles; S – sacks

COWBOYS PLAYOFF STATISTICS

APPENDIX Ib

TEAM

	Dallas	Opponents
Total First Downs	66	58
Rushing	26	20
Passing	38	33
Penalty	2	5
3rd Down Made-Att.	19-36	10-30
3rd Down Efficiency	52.8	33.3
4th Down Made-Att.	0.0	40.0
Total Net Yards	1170	955
Total offensive plays	193	182
Avg. gain per play	6.1	5.2
Net Yards Rushing	418	285
Total rushing plays	97	67
Avg. gain per rush	4.3	4.3
Net Yards Passing	752	670
Sacks-yards lost	7-43	12-79
Gross yards passing	795	749
Attempts	89	103
Completions	61	64
Had Intercepted	0	6
Avg. gain per pass	8.4	6.5
Punts-Average	11-40.5	11-43.5
Had blocked	1	0
Return Yards	118	54
Punt returns-yards	6-48	8-54
Int. returns-yards	6-70	0-0
Kickoff returns-yards	10-212	15-314
Penalties-Yards	17-108	14-144
Fumbles-no. lost	7-3	14-9
Touchdowns	15	5
Rushing	5	2
Passing	8	3
Return	2	0
Extra Point Made-Att.	14-15	5-5
Field Goals Made-Att.	4-5	4-5
Avg. Time of Possession	34:16	25:44

COWBOYS SEASON IN REVIEW

APPENDIX IIa

PRE-SEASON (2-3)

Date	Opponent	Result	Attendance (no-shows)	Record
Sat., Aug. 1	Houston-a	L 34-23	51,158 (n/a)	0-1
Fri., Aug. 7	at Miami	W 27-24	50,803 (n/a)	1-1
Sat., Aug. 15	Houston	L 17-16	61,334 (n/a)	1-2
Sat., Aug. 22	Denver	W 17-3	61,485 (n/a)	2-2
Fri., Aug. 28	Chicago	L 20-13	60,218 (n/a)	2-3

a-at Tokyo Dome

REGULAR SEASON (13-3)

Date	Opponent	Result	Attendance (no-shows)	Record
Mon., Sept. 7	Washington	W 23-10	63,538 (1,484)	1-0
Sun., Sept. 13	at NY Giants	W 34-28	76,430 (766)	2-0
Sun., Sept. 20	Phoenix	W 31-20	62,575 (2,447)	3-0
Mon., Oct. 5	at Philadelphia	L 31-7	66,572 (243)	3-1
Sun., Oct. 11	Seattle	W 27-0	62,311 (2,711)	4-1
Sun., Oct. 18	Kansas City	W 17-10	64,115 (907)	5-1
Sun., Oct. 25	at LA Raiders	W 28-13	91,505 (983)	6-1
Sun., Nov. 1	Philadelphia	W 20-10	65,012 (10)	7-1
Sun., Nov. 8	at Detroit	W 37-3	74,816 (5,338)	8-1
Sun., Nov. 15	LA Rams	L 27-23	63,690 (1,332)	8-2
Sun., Nov. 22	at Phoenix	W 16-10	72,439 (510)	9-2
Thu., Nov. 26	NY Giants	W 30-3	62,416 (2,608)	10-2
Sun., Dec. 6	at Denver	W 31-27	74,946 (1,121)	11-2
Sun., Dec. 13	at Washington	L 20-17	56,437 (17)	11-3
Mon., Dec. 21	at Atlanta	W 41-17	67,036 (4,088)	12-3
Sun., Dec. 27	Chicago	W 27-14	63,101 (1,921)	13-3

PLAYOFFS (3-0)

Date	Opponent	Result	Attendance (no-shows)	Record
Sun., Jan. 10	Philadelphia	W 34-10	63,721 (1,303)	14-3
Sun., Jan. 17	at San Francisco	W 30-20	64,920 (1,444)	15-3
Sun., Jan. 31	Buffalo-b	W 52-17	98,374 (0)	16-3

b-at Rose Bowl, Pasadena, Calif.

NFL PLAYOFFS

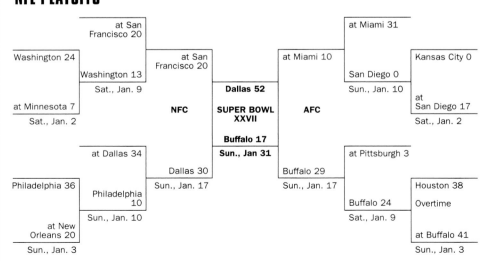

1992 SINGLE-GAME BESTS
REGULAR SEASON:
- **Yards rushing:** 174, Emmitt Smith at Atlanta, Dec. 21.
- **Rushing attempts:** 30, Emmitt Smith vs. Phialdelphia, Nov. 1.
- **Rushing touchdowns:** 3, Emmitt Smith at Los Angeles Raiders, Nov. 1, and at Detroit, Nov. 8.
- **Longest rush:** 68, Emmitt Smith vs. New York Giants, Nov. 26.
- **Yards passing:** 272, Troy Aikman vs. Los Angeles Rams, Nov. 15.
- **Passing attempts:** 38, Troy Aikman at Philadelphia, Oct. 5.
- **Passes completed:** 25, Troy Aikman vs. Los Angeles Rams, Nov. 15.
- **Passing touchdowns:** 3, Troy Aikman, three times; last time at Atlanta, Dec. 21.
- **Yards receiving:** 210, Michael Irvin vs. Phoenix, Sept. 20.
- **Receptions:** 12, Emmitt Smith at Phoenix, Nov. 22.
- **Receiving touchdowns:** 3, Michael Irvin vs. Phoenix, Sept. 20.
- **Longest reception:** 87, Michael Irvin vs. Phoenix, Sept. 20.
- **Field goals:** 3, Lin Elliott, three times; last time vs. New York Giants, Nov. 26.
- **Longest field goal:** 53, Lin Elliott vs. New York Giants, Nov. 26, and at Denver, Dec. 6.
- **Longest punt:** 58, Mike Saxon vs. Phoenix, Sept. 20.
- **Interceptions:** 2, Thomas Everett at Detroit, Nov. 8.
- **Sacks:** 2, seven times, last by Charles Haley at Atlanta, Dec. 21.
- **Solo tackles:** 10, Robert Jones at Philadelphia, Oct. 5.
- **Combined tackles:** 16, Robert Jones at Philadelphia, Oct. 5, and vs. Kansas City, Oct. 18.

INDIVIDUAL RECORDS TIED IN 1992
REGULAR SEASON:
- **Fewest games 1,000 yards rushing, season:** 10, Emmitt Smith.
- **Consecutive games 100 yards receiving:** 3, Michael Irvin.
- **Fair catches, season:** 18, Kelvin Martin.
- **Punt return touchdowns, season:** 2, Kelvin Martin.
- **Kick return touchdowns, career:** 3, Kelvin Martin.
- **Combined kick return touchdowns, season:** 2, Kelvin Martin.

TEAM RECORDS IN 1992
REGULAR SEASON:
BROKEN
- **Most games won:** 13.
- **Most points scored, third quarter:** 24 vs. Chicago, Dec. 27.
- **Fewest first downs rushing, opponent 16-game season:** 68.
- **Fewest yards gained, opponent 16-game season:** 3,933.
- **Fewest yards gained, opponent game:** 62 vs. Seattle, Oct. 11,
- **Fewest rushing attempts, opponent 16-game season:** 345.
- **Fewest rushing attempts, game:** 11 at Atlanta, Dec. 21.
- **Fewest yards rushing, opponent 16-game season:** 1,244.
- **Completion percentage, season:** 64.0.
- **Fewest sacks allowed, season:** 23.
- **Fewest sack yards allowed, season:** 112.
- **Highest attempts-sack ratio, season:** 22.4.
- **Fewest fumbles, season:** 16.

TIED
- **Fewest first downs rushing, opponent, game:** 0 at Phoenix, Nov. 22.
- **Fewest first downs by penalty, season:** 22.
- **Games with no sacks allowed, season:** 5.
- **Most touchdowns, punt return, season:** 2.
- **Consecutive games without losing a fumble:** 4.
- **Fewest fumbles lost, season:** 9.

SINGLE-GAME PLAYOFF RECORDS
BROKEN
- **Completion percentage (min. 15 attempts):** 73.3, Troy Aikman vs. Buffalo, Jan. 31.
- **Most points scored, combined:** 69, Jan. 31, Dallas 52, Buffalo 17.
- **Most fumbles, opponent:** 8, by Buffalo, Jan. 31.
- **Most fumbles lost, opponent:** 5, by Buffalo, Jan. 31.

TIED
- **Extra points attempted-made:** 7, Lin Elliott, Jan. 31 vs. Buffalo.
- **Touchdown passes:** 4, Troy Aikman, Jan. 31 vs. Buffalo.
- **Most points scored:** 52, Jan. 31 vs. Buffalo.
- **Most first downs by penalty, opponent:** 4, Jan. 31 vs. Buffalo.

COWBOYS SEASON RECORDS

APPENDIX IIb

COWBOYS ROSTER
JULY 27, 1992

APPENDIX IIIa

No.	Name	Position	Height	Weight	Age	Exp.	College	How acquired
1	Green, Anthony	WR	5-11	190	25	1	W. Kentucky	FA-'92
2	Elliott, Lin	K	6-0	180	23	R	Texas Tech	FA-'92
4	Saxon, Mike	P	6-3	202	30	8	San Diego St.	FA-'92
5	Daluiso, Brad	K	6-2	207	25	2	UCLA	PB(Buf)-'92
6	Smith, Jimmy	WR	6-1	200	23	R	Jackson State	D2a-'92
7	Beuerlein, Steve	QB	6-2	209	27	5	Notre Dame	T(Raid)-'91
8	Aikman, Troy	QB	6-4	222	25	4	UCLA	D1-'89
9	Kupp, Craig	QB	6-4	215	25	2	Pacific Luth.	W(Pho)-'91
17	Garrett, Jason	QB	6-2	195	26	1	Princeton	FA-'92
19	James, Michael	DB	5-11	184	23	R	Arkansas	FA-92
20	Horton, Ray	S	5-11	190	32	10	Washington	PB(Cin)-'89
21	Lewis, Garry	CB	5-11	185	24	3	Alcorn State	T(Raid)-'92
22	Smith, Emmitt	RB	5-9	203	23	3	Florida	D1-'90
23	Williams, Robert	DB	5-10	190	29	6	Baylor	FA-'87
24	Brown, Larry	CB	5-11	182	22	2	TCU	D12-'91
25	Mitchell, Brian	CB	5-9	164	23	2	Brigham Young	PB(Atl)-'92
26	Smith, Kevin	CB	5-11	173	22	R	Texas A&M	D1a-'92
27	Richards, Curvin	RB	5-9	195	23	1	Pittsburgh	D4a-'92
28	Weatherspoon, Chuck	RB	5-7	229	23	2	Houston	FA-'92
29	Gant, Kenneth	DB	5-11	188	25	3	Albany State	D9-'90
30	Holt, Issiac	CB	6-2	201	29	8	Alcorn State	T(Min)-'89
31	Harris, Donald	S	6-0	185	24	R	Texas Tech	D12-'92
32	Brooks, Michael	S	6-0	189	25	2	N.C. State	FA-'90
33	Burse, Tony	RB	6-0	218	27	2	Mid. Tenn. St.	FA-'92
34	Agee, Tommie	FB	6-0	225	27	5	Auburn	PB(KC)-'90
35	Jordan, Tony	RB	6-2	220	27	3	Kansas State	FA-'92
37	Washington, James	S	6-1	197	27	5	UCLA	PB(Rams)-'90
38	Hall, Chris	S	6-2	184	22	R	East Carolina	D9b-'92
40	Bates, Bill	S	6-1	205	31	10	Tennessee	FA-'83
41	Beasley, Michael	RB	5-10	203	23	R	West Virginia	FA-'92
43	Bartlewski, Rich	TE	6-4	239	24	2	Fresno State	FA-'92
45	Woodson, Darren	S	6-1	216	23	R	Arizona State	D2b-'92
47	Holmes, Clayton	CB	5-10	178	22	R	Carson-Newman	D3a-'92
48	Johnston, Daryl	FB	6-2	236	26	4	Syracuse	D2-'92
49	Hillman, Jay	FB	6-0	220	24	R	Boston Univ.	FA-'92
50	Crum, Maurice	LB	6-0	220	23	1	Miami, Fla.	FA-'92
51	Norton, Ken	LB	6-2	238	25	5	UCLA	D2-'88
52	Pruitt, Mickey	LB	6-1	218	27	5	Colorado	W(Chi)-'91
53	Stepnoski, Mark	C	6-2	269	25	4	Pittsburgh	D3a-'89
55	Jones, Robert	LB	6-2	236	22	R	East Carolina	D1b-'92
57	Smith, Vinson	LB	6-2	231	27	4	East Carolina	PB(Pit)-'90
58	Edwards, Dixon	LB	6-1	224	24	2	Michigan St.	D2-'91
59	Clark, Bernard	LB	6-2	248	25	3	Miami, Fla.	PB(Cin)-'92
60	Evans, Melvin	OL	6-2	316	23	2	Tex. Southern	FA-'92
61	Newton, Nate	T	6-3	332	30	7	Florida A&M	FA-'86
62	Terry, John	OL	6-4	292	23	R	Livingstone	D10-'92
63	Gesek, John	G	6-5	279	29	6	Cal. St. Sacramento	T(Raid)-'90
64	Myslinski, Tom	G	6-2	291	23	R	Tennessee	D4-'92
65	Milstead, Rod	G	6-2	293	22	R	Delaware St.	D5b-'92
66	Gogan, Kevin	G	6-7	317	27	6	Washington	D8-'87
67	Maryland, Russell	DT	6-1	272	23	2	Miami, Fla.	D1a-'91
68	Cornish, Frank	OL	6-4	295	24	3	UCLA	PB(SD)-'92
70	Hellestrae, Dale	OL	6-5	285	30	6	SMU	T(Raid)-'90
71	Tuinei, Mark	T	6-5	299	32	10	Hawaii	FA-'83
72	Evans, Patt	TE	6-6	261	23	R	Minnesota	FA-'92
73	Noonan, Danny	DT	6-4	275	27	6	Nebraska	D1-'87
74	Brown, James	T	6-6	331	22	R	Virginia St.	D3b-'92
75	Casillas, Tony	DT	6-3	277	28	7	Oklahoma	T(Atl)-'91
76	Veingrad, Alan	OL	6-5	280	29	6	E. Texas St.	PB(GB)-'91
77	Jeffcoat, Jim	DE	6-5	274	31	10	Arizona State	D1-'83
78	Lett, Leon	DL	6-6	287	23	2	Emporia State	D7-'91
79	Williams, Erik	T	6-6	319	23	2	Central St.	D3c-'91
80	Harper, Alvin	WR	6-3	203	25	2	Tennessee	D1b-'91
81	Wright, Alexander	WR	6-0	190	25	3	Auburn	D2-'90
82	Shepard, Derrick	WR	5-10	183	28	5	Oklahoma	FA-'91
83	Martin, Kelvin	WR	5-9	162	27	6	Boston Col.	D4-'87
84	Novacek, Jay	TE	6-4	231	29	8	Wyoming	PB(Pho)-'90
85	Lomack, Tony	WR	5-8	180	24	2	Florida	FA-'92
86	Alphin, Gerald	WR	6-3	220	28	3	Kansas State	FA-'92
87	Roberts, Alfredo	TE	6-3	252	27	5	Miami, Fla.	PB(KC)-'91
88	Irvin, Michael	WR	6-2	199	26	5	Miami, Fla.	D1-'88
89	Wacasey, Fallon	TE	6-7	241	23	R	Tulsa	D6-'92
90	Hill, Tony	DE	6-6	242	23	2	Tenn.-Chat.	D4c-'91
91	Butts, Anthony	DT	6-4	300	25	1	Miss. St.	FA-'92
92	Tolbert, Tony	DE	6-6	265	24	4	UT-El Paso	D4-'89
93	Cooper, Reggie	LB	6-2	215	24	2	Nebraska	FA-'91
94	Harris, Kevin	DE	6-5	251	22	1	Tex. Southern	D4d-'91
95	Hennings, Chad	DE	6-6	272	26	R	Air Force	D11-'88
96	Burch, Swift	DL	6-4	272	23	R	Temple	FA-'92
97	Jones, Jimmie	DL	6-4	276	26	3	Miami, Fla.	D3-'90
98	Myles, Godfrey	LB	6-1	241	23	2	Florida	D3a-'91

RESERVE/PHYSICALLY UNABLE TO PERFORM

No.	Name	Position	Height	Weight	Age	Exp.	College	How acquired
3	Daniel, Tim (right hamstring)	WR	5-11	184	22	R	Florida A&M	D11-'92
42	Briggs, Greg (right hip)	S	6-3	209	23	R	Tex. Southern	D5a-'92
46	Blake, Ricky (right hip)	RB	6-2	244	25	2	Alabama A&M	FA-'91
56	Foster, Melvin (right knee)	LB	6-1	243	25	R	Iowa	FA-'92
69	Jones, Todd (left knee)	G	6-3	295	25	1	Henderson St.	FA-'92

FA – signed as free agent
PB – signed as Plan B free agent
D – drafted
W – claimed on waivers
T – acquired in trade

Feb. 1: Acquired cornerback Garry Lewis from Los Angeles Raiders for seventh-round draft choice.

Feb. 10: Kicker Ken Willis (Plan B) signed with Tampa Bay.

Feb. 11: Signed running back Tony Boles.

Feb. 13: Signed kicker Brad Daluiso (Plan B) and linebacker Maurice Crum.

March 3: Linebacker Jack Del Rio (Plan B) signed with Minnesota.

March 9: Signed running back Chuck Weatherspoon.

March 11: Linebacker Darrick Brownlow (Plan B) signed with Buffalo; signed linebacker Bernard Clark (Plan B).

March 13: Signed running back Lorenzo Graham.

March 23: Signed quarterback Jason Garrett.

March 27: Signed wide receiver Gerald Alphin and cornerback Brian Mitchell (Plan B).

March 30: Defensive back Stan Smagala (Plan B) signed with Pittsburgh.

March 31: Tight end Rob Awalt (Plan B) signed with Denver.

April 1: Signed offensive lineman Frank Cornish (Plan B); cornerback Manny Hendrix (Plan B) signed with San Francisco.

April 7: Signed running back Tony Jordan.

April 8: Signed wide receiver Tony Lomack.

April 26: Drafted cornerback Kevin Smith, linebacker Robert Jones, wide receiver Jimmy Smith, safety Darren Woodson, cornerback Clayton Holmes, offensive tackle James Brown, guard Tom Myslinski, safety Greg Briggs and guard Rod Milstead; signed Kevin Smith, Woodson and Holmes.

April 27: Drafted tight end Fallon Wacasey, safety Nate Kirtman, safety Chris Hall, offensive lineman John Terry, wide receiver Tim Daniel and safety Donald Harris.

April 28: Signed running back Michael Beasley, defensive lineman Swift Burch, guard Melvin Evans, tight end Patt Evans, tight end Harold Heath, safety Michael James and linebacker Terry Tilton.

April 29: Signed kicker Lin Elliott; acquired running back Keith Woodside from Green Bay for an undisclosed draft choice.

May 1: Running back Keith Woodside failed physical, voiding April 29 trade; linebacker Terry Tilton failed physical.

June 1: Signed wide receiver Derrick Shepard.

June 3: Signed tight end Rich Bartlewski.

June 4: Signed linebacker Melvin Foster.

June 10: Signed safety Greg Briggs and guard Todd Jones.

June 15: Signed running back Tony Burse.

June 16: Signed defensive tackle Anthony Butts.

July 8: Released safety Vince Albritton.

July 13: Signed tight end Fallon Wacasey.

July 14: Signed fullback Jay Hillman.

July 15: Signed safety Bill Bates, offensive lineman James Brown, wide receiver Tim Daniel, safety Chris Hall, safety Nate Kirtman, guard Rod Milstead, guard Tom Myslinski and offensive lineman John Terry.

July 16: Signed safety Ray Horton; placed running back Ricky Blake, safety Greg Briggs, wide receiver Tim Daniel, linebacker Melvin Foster and guard Todd Jones on physically unable to perform list.

July 22: Signed cornerback Garry Lewis.

July 26: Released fullback Lorenzo Graham, tight end Harold Heath and safety Nate Kirtman.

July 27: Signed safety Donald Harris.

Aug. 3: Released safety Michael Brooks.

Aug. 4: Signed linebacker Vinson Smith.

Aug. 5: Released defensive lineman Swift Burch.

Aug. 6: Signed defensive end Jim Jeffcoat.

Aug. 10: Released running back Tony Burse and running back Tony Jordan.

Aug. 11: Signed safety James Washington.

Aug. 12: Signed linebacker Ken Norton.

Aug. 17: Released offensive lineman James Brown, safety Donald Harris and safety Michael James.

Aug. 23: Signed defensive end Tony Tolbert.

Aug. 24: Traded guard Rod Milstead to Cleveland for an undisclosed 1993 draft choice.

Aug. 24: Released defensive tackle Anthony Butts, linebacker Bernard Clark, tight end Patt Evans, wide receiver Anthony Green, safety Chris Hall, fullback Jay Hillman and offensive lineman John Terry.

Aug. 26: Acquired tight end Chad Fortune off waivers from Washington; released cornerback Brian Mitchell.

Aug. 27: Traded cornerback Garry Lewis to Tampa Bay for a ninth-round 1993 draft choice; acquired defensive end Charles Haley from San Francisco for undisclosed 1993 draft choices.

Aug. 30: Signed tight end Jay Novacek; released kicker Brad Daluiso.

Aug. 31: Released wide receiver Gerald Alphin, running back Michael Beasley, linebacker Reggie Cooper, linebacker Maurice Crum, tight end Chad Fortune, quarterback Jason Garrett, defensive end Kevin Harris, offensive lineman Dale Hellestrae, quarterback Craig Kupp, wide receiver Tony Lomack, guard Tom Myslinski, wide receiver Derrick Shepard, tight end Fallon Wacasey and running back Chuck Weatherspoon.

Sept. 1: Claimed linebacker Bobby Abrams off waivers from New York Giants; released tight end Rich Bartlewski and linebacker Mickey Pruitt; signed running back Michael Beasley, quarterback Jason Garrett, guard Tom Myslinski and tight end Fallon Wacasey to practice squad.

Sept. 2: Re-signed offensive lineman Dale Hellestrae; placed defensive end Tony Hill and wide receiver Jimmy Smith on injured reserve; took tight end Jay Novacek and defensive end Tony Tolbert off exempt list; signed wide receiver Tyrone Williams to practice squad.

Sept. 3: Signed wide receiver Michael Irvin.

Sept. 4: Placed guard Melvin Evans on injured reserve.

Sept. 5: Signed center Mark Stepnoski.

Sept. 8: Guard Tom Myslinski signed off practice squad by Cleveland; signed tight end Patt Evans to practice squad.

Sept. 14: Released defensive tackle Danny Noonan; removed center Mark Stepnoski from exempt list.

Sept. 19: Acquired safety Thomas Everett from Pittsburgh for an undisclosed draft choice.

Sept. 21: Placed running back Curvin Richards and cornerback Robert Williams on injured reserve.

Sept. 26: Released tight end Patt Evans from practice squad.

Sept. 28: Activated defensive end Tony Hill from injured reserve (free move); counted Jimmy Smith (IR) on practice squad.

Sept. 30: Signed tight end Patt Evans to practice squad.

Oct. 6: Released linebacker Bobby Abrams.

Oct. 7: Activated wide receiver Jimmy Smith from injured reserve (free move); counted Melvin Evans (IR) on practice squad.

Oct. 12: Traded wide receiver Alexander Wright to Los Angeles Raiders for an undisclosed draft choice.

Oct. 14: Placed safety Bill Bates on injured reserve.

Oct. 15: Signed running back Derrick Gainer.

Oct. 19: Released running back Ricky Blake from physically unable to perform list; counted running back Curvin Richards (IR) on practice squad; removed guard Melvin Evans (IR) from practice squad.

Oct. 23: Activated running back Curvin Richards (free move); counted guard Melvin Evans (IR) on practice squad.

Oct. 26: Placed safety Ray Horton on injured reserve; counted cornerback Robert Williams (IR) on practice squad; removed guard Melvin Evans (IR) from practice squad.

Oct. 29: Placed cornerback Robert Williams on recall waivers, claimed by Phoenix.

Nov. 2: Counted guard Melvin Evans (IR) on practice squad.

Nov. 3: Re-signed cornerback Robert Williams.

Nov. 17: Placed defensive end Tony Hill on injured reserve.

Nov. 18: Re-signed linebacker Mickey Pruitt.

Nov. 23: Activated safety Ray Horton (free move); placed running back Derrick Gainer on injured reserve.

Dec. 28: Released running back Curvin Richards; activated running back Derrick Gainer (free move).

Dec. 29: Signed tight end Derek Tennell; removed guard Melvin Evans (IR) from practice squad; signed tight end Milton Biggins to practice squad.

COWBOYS ROSTER
JAN. 31, 1993

APPENDIX IIIc

HEAD COACH
- Jimmy Johnson

ASSISTANT COACHES
- Dave Wannstedt (assistant head coach/ defensive coordinator/linebackers)
- Norv Turner (offensive coordinator/ quarterbacks)
- Hubbard Alexander (receivers)
- Joe Avezzano (special teams)
- Joe Brodsky (running backs)
- Dave Campo (defensive backs)
- Butch Davis (defensive line)
- Robert Ford (tight ends)
- Steve Hoffman (kickers/quality control)
- Bob Slowik (defensive assistant)
- Tony Wise (offensive line)
- Mike Woicik (strength and conditioning)

No.	Name	Position	Height	Weight	Age	Exp.	College	How acquired
2	Elliott, Lin	K	6-0	182	24	R	Texas Tech	FA-'92
4	Saxon, Mike	P	6-3	200	30	8	San Diego St.	FA-'92
7	Beuerlein, Steve	QB	6-2	213	27	5	Notre Dame	T(Raid)-'91
8	Aikman, Troy	QB	6-4	222	26	4	UCLA	D1-'89
20	Horton, Ray	S	5-11	188	32	10	Washington	PB(Cin)-'89
22	Smith, Emmitt	RB	5-9	209	23	3	Florida	D1-'90
23	Williams, Robert	S	5-10	186	30	6	Baylor	FA-'87
24	Brown, Larry	CB	5-11	185	23	2	TCU	D12-'91
26	Smith, Kevin	CB	5-11	177	22	R	Texas A&M	D1a-'92
27	Everett, Thomas	S	5-9	183	28	6	Baylor	T(Pit)-'92
28	Woodson, Darren	S	6-1	215	23	R	Arizona State	D2b-'92
29	Gant, Kenneth	DB	5-11	191	25	3	Albany State	D9-'90
30	Holt, Issiac	CB	6-2	198	30	8	Alcorn State	T(Min)-'89
34	Agee, Tommie	FB	6-0	227	28	5	Auburn	PB(KC)-'90
37	Washington, James	S	6-1	203	28	5	UCLA	PB(Rams)-'90
39	Gainer, Derrick	RB	5-11	240	26	2	Florida A&M	FA-'92
47	Holmes, Clayton	CB	5-10	181	23	R	Carson-Newman	D3a-'92
48	Johnston, Daryl	FB	6-2	238	26	4	Syracuse	D2-'89
51	Norton, Ken	LB	6-2	241	26	5	UCLA	D2-'88
52	Pruitt, Mickey	LB	6-1	218	28	5	Colorado	W(Chi)-'91
53	Stepnoski, Mark	C	6-2	269	25	4	Pittsburgh	D3a-'89
55	Jones, Robert	LB	6-2	238	23	R	East Carolina	D1b-'92
57	Smith, Vinson	LB	6-2	237	27	4	East Carolina	PB(Pit)-'90
58	Edwards, Dixon	LB	6-1	224	24	2	Michigan St.	D2-'91
61	Newton, Nate	T	6-3	303	31	7	Florida A&M	FA-'86
63	Gesek, John	G	6-5	282	29	6	Cal. St. Sacramento	T(Raid)-'90
66	Gogan, Kevin	G	6-7	319	28	6	Washington	D8-'87
67	Maryland, Russell	DT	6-1	275	23	2	Miami, Fla.	D1a-'91
68	Cornish, Frank	OL	6-4	285	25	3	UCLA	PB(SD)-'92
70	Hellestrae, Dale	OL	6-5	283	30	6	SMU	T(Raid)-'90
71	Tuinei, Mark	T	6-5	298	32	10	Hawaii	FA-'83
75	Casillas, Tony	DT	6-3	273	29	7	Oklahoma	T(Atl)-'91
76	Veingrad, Alan	OL	6-5	280	29	6	E. Texas St.	PB(GB)-'91
77	Jeffcoat, Jim	DE	6-5	276	31	10	Arizona State	D1-'83
78	Lett, Leon	DL	6-6	292	24	2	Emporia State	D7-'91
79	Williams, Erik	T	6-6	321	24	2	Central St.	D3c-'91
80	Harper, Alvin	WR	6-3	207	25	2	Tennessee	D1b-'91
82	Smith, Jimmy	WR	6-1	205	23	R	Jackson State	D2a-'92
83	Martin, Kelvin	WR	5-9	165	27	6	Boston Col.	D4-'87
84	Novacek, Jay	TE	6-4	231	30	8	Wyoming	PB(Pho)-'90
88	Irvin, Michael	WR	6-2	199	26	5	Miami, Fla.	D1-'88
89	Tennell, Derek	TE	6-5	270	28	5	UCLA	FA-'92
92	Tolbert, Tony	DE	6-6	265	25	4	UT-El Paso	D4-'89
94	Haley, Charles	DE	6-5	245	29	7	James Madison	T(SF)-'92
95	Hennings, Chad	DE	6-6	267	27	R	Air Force	D11-'88
97	Jones, Jimmie	DL	6-4	276	27	3	Miami, Fla.	D3-'90
98	Myles, Godfrey	LB	6-1	242	24	2	Florida	D3a-'91

RESERVE/INJURED

No.	Name	Position	Height	Weight	Age	Exp.	College	How acquired
90	Hill, Tony (right hamstring, Nov. 18)	DE	6-6	255	24	2	Tenn.-Chat.	D4c-'91
40	Bates, Bill (left knee, Oct. 12)	S	6-1	203	31	10	Tennessee	FA-'83
60	Evans, Melvin (left ankle, Sept. 4)	OL	6-2	303	23	R	Tex. Southern	FA-'9
87	Roberts, Alfredo (right knee, Dec. 29)	TE	6-3	251	27	5	Miami, Fla.	PB(KC)-'91

RESERVE/PHYSICALLY UNABLE TO PERFORM

No.	Name	Position	Height	Weight	Age	Exp.	College	How acquired
	Briggs, Greg (right hip, Aug. 25)	S	6-3	212	24	R	Tex. Southern	D5a-'92
	Daniel, Tim (right hamstring, Aug. 25)	WR	5-11	192	23	R	Florida A&M	D11-'92
	Foster, Melvin (right knee, Aug. 25)	LB	6-1	247	26	R	Iowa	FA-'92
	Jones, Todd (left knee, Aug. 25)	G	6-3	295	25	1	Henderson St.	FA-'92

PRACTICE SQUAD

No.	Name	Position	Height	Weight	Age	Exp.	College	How acquired
	Beasley, Michael	RB	5-10	195	23	R	West Virginia	FA-'92
	Biggins, Milton	TE	6-4	273	23	R	W. Kentucky	FA-'92
	Evans, Patt	TE	6-6	261	23	R	Minnesota	FA-'92
	Garrett, Jason	QB	6-2	195	26	1	Princeton	FA-'92
	Wacasey, Fallon	TE	6-7	263	23	R	Tulsa	D6-'92
	Williams, Tyrone	WR	6-5	207	22	R	W. Ontario	FA-'92

FA – signed as free agent
PB – signed as Plan B free agent
D – drafted
W – claimed on waivers
T – acquired in trade

FROM THE DRAFT (26):

1983: Jim Jeffcoat (1st, Arizona State)
1987: Kelvin Martin (4th, Boston College)
Kevin Gogan (8th, Washington)
1988: Michael Irvin (1st, Miami)
Ken Norton (2nd, UCLA)
Chad Hennings (11th, Air Force)
1989: Troy Aikman (1st, UCLA)
Daryl Johnston (2nd, Syracuse)
Mark Stepnoski (3rd, Pittsburgh)
Tony Tolbert (4th, UT-El Paso)
1990: Emmitt Smith (1st, Florida)
Jimmie Jones (3rd, Miami)
Kenneth Gant (9th, Albany State)

1991: Russell Maryland (1st, Miami)
Alvin Harper (1st, Tennessee)
Dixon Edwards (2nd, Michigan State)
Godfrey Myles (3rd, Florida)
Erik Williams (3rd, Central State, Ohio)
Tony Hill* (4th, Tennessee-Chattanooga)
Leon Lett (7th, Emporia State, Kansas)
Larry Brown (12th, TCU).
1992: Kevin Smith (1st, Texas A&M)
Robert Jones (1st, East Carolina)
Jimmy Smith (2nd, Jackson State)
Darren Woodson (2nd, Arizona State)
Clayton Holmes (3rd, Carson-Newman)

SIGNED AS FREE AGENTS (18):

1983: Bill Bates* (Tennessee)
Mark Tuinei (Hawaii).
1985: Mike Saxon (San Diego State)
1986: Nate Newton (Florida A&M)
1987: Robert Williams (Baylor)
1989: b-Ray Horton (Washington)
1990: b-Tommie Agee (Auburn)
b-Jay Novacek (Wyoming)
b-Vinson Smith (East Carolina)
b-James Washington (UCLA)

1991: b-Alfredo Roberts* (Miami)
b-Alan Veingrad (East Texas State)
1992: b-Frank Cornish (UCLA)
Lin Elliott (Texas Tech)
Melvin Evans* (Texas Southern)
Derrick Gainer (Florida A&M)
Mickey Pruitt (Colorado)
Derek Tennell (Western Kentucky)

IN TRADES (7):

1989: Issiac Holt (Alcorn State, from Minnesota
in Herschel Walker trade).
1990: John Gesek (Cal-State Sacramento, from
Los Angeles Raiders for 1991 fifth-round pick)
Dale Hellestrae (SMU, from Los Angeles
Raiders for 1991 seventh-round pick in 1991)
1991: Steve Beuerlein (Notre Dame, from Los
Angeles Raiders for 1992 fourth-round pick)

Tony Casillas (Oklahoma, from Atlanta for
1992 second- and eighth-round picks in 1992)
1992: Charles Haley (James Madison, from San
Francisco for undisclosed draft choices)
Thomas Everett (Baylor, from Pittsburgh
for undisclosed 1993 draft choice)

* Injured reserve
b – Plan B free agent

HOW THE COWBOYS WERE BUILT

APPENDIX IIId

IRWIN THOMPSON